The True Herod

The True Herod

Geza Vermes

B L O O M S B U R Y

LONDON · NEW DELHI · NEW YORK · SYDNEY

Bloomsbury T&T Clark

An imprint of Bloomsbury Publishing Plc

50 Bedford Square   1385 Broadway
London   New York
WC1B 3DP   NY 10018
UK   USA

www.bloomsbury.com

Bloomsbury is a registered trade mark of Bloomsbury Publishing Plc

First published 2014

© Geza Vermes, 2014

British Library Cataloguing-in-Publication Data
A catalogue record for this book is available from the British Library.

ISBN: HB: 978–0–56757–544–9
ePDF: 978–0–56748–841–1
ePub: 978–0–56718–657–7

Library of Congress Cataloging-in-Publication Data

Vermes, Geza
The True Herod/ Geza Vermes p.cm
Includes bibliographic references and index.
ISBN 978-0-5675-7544-9 (hardcover)

Typeset by RefineCatch Limited, Bungay, Suffolk
Printed and bound in India

Contents

Foreword

The origin of this book was not centred on one idea but a myriad of unstructured tales and loose ends that grew into one story. *The True Herod* is very special to me as it is published after the death of my late husband and is full of memories. It was neither commissioned, nor the result of serious study, unlike most of his other books, and it took years of story-telling and good fortune to grow into a publication. The stories, accounts and snippets contained in this volume accompanied our life together for many years; he told them to entertain me whether on rainy trips to London or sunny journeys towards the Mediterranean. I remember him announcing, with a twinkle in his eyes, 'Darling, now we are heading towards civilisation' as we crossed the bridge over the Loire before launching into another bawdy encounter between Cleopatra and Herod.

The lives of the major Roman, Jewish and Egyptian players from the time of Jesus had intertwined relationships, and their respective cultures rubbed against each other. But in tying this period together, Geza saw Herod as one of the pivotal axes around which his contemporaries revolved. Despite being mostly negatively portrayed, and seldom debated, he does not make for a poor hero; for beyond the treachery and violence, his power and passion brought peace and prosperity. It was these misconceptions that Geza loved to challenge, and thus the book was born, or at least the main part of it. However, for some time it lay quietly on his desk and, for various reasons, it sank to the bottom of the pile.

In early January 2013, on a day when a sudden snowfall had paralysed Oxford and brought the rest of Britain to a standstill, a young and friendly editor from Bloomsbury arrived at our doorstep perfectly on time, impressing Geza, who had been anxious the man would not appear. While they discussed revisiting an earlier publication, the conversation happily turned to new ideas and by the warmth of the fireside, the dust from *The True Herod* was blown off. That evening, he informed us from a coach to London that he was the sole passenger but also that he would take on the book. I suspect, though cold and alone, he was as jubilant as the author. Geza set to work the next morning, and the manuscript grew until it was finished on 31st March. I later noticed, while editing this book, some final adjustments had been made to the digital files just four days before Geza died. He passed away peacefully from a complication of his chemotherapy on the 8th May 2013.

Geza's writing has the ability to surprise us, to nourish our imagination and to touch us, leaving us with something that stays forever. I hope this book will provide the readers with some colourful and inspiring glimpses into this other world.

15th December 2013   Margaret Vermes

Preface

For many years I have been fascinated by the figure of Herod the Great (c. 73–4 BCE). Having read and re-read Josephus' accounts in the *Jewish War* and *Antiquities*, and having attempted to discount the pro-Herodian and pro-Hasmonaean bias in the two works, I easily reached the conclusion that both the Christian and the Jewish rabbinic traditions have faced us with a caricature of the true Herod. Herod was not an enemy of the Jews, nor was he guilty of the massacre of the babes in Bethlehem as the evangelist Matthew would like his readers to believe. He was heroic and horrible. A genius in politics as well as a giant in architecture and planning, he was at the same time shamefully vindictive towards those he considered potential rivals or opponents, including the close members of his family. He was a typical split personality and his two opposite qualities turned him into a genuine tragic hero. It is amazing that no top class filmmaker has yet discovered these latent potentials and raised him to stardom as they did with his classical contemporaries, Julius Caesar and Antony and Cleopatra. No doubt they were unable to recognize that the lens of the Christian tradition provided them with a grossly distorted image of the real Herod.

However, a good historian should not allow Herod's generally known weaknesses to obscure his greatness, nor the negative aspects of his complex personality to obfuscate his brilliant and, yes, I will dare say it, his kindness and generosity towards his subjects, Jewish and non-Jewish, in their hours of need. As a recent writer aptly put it, appropriating Graham Greene's formula, Herod was truly 'the *Third* Man' in the Roman Empire of his age, who was preceded only by Augustus and his best friend, Agrippa, with the King of the Jews being the next best and influential friend of both.

In this richly illustrated account, Herod and his successors down to the third generation are set within the framework of Jewish and Graeco-Roman history, with a bird's eye view back to the age of David (c. 1000 BCE) and a forward look to the aftermath of the Jewish rebellion against Rome in the final decades of the first century CE. The book is meant for all and sundry, with no prior requirement beyond a basic education. I hope the readers will find the pages and pictures that follow instructive and entertaining, in short, a good read.

Oxford, 31st March 2013   Geza Vermes

Acknowledgements

While finalizing the manuscript last March we learnt that a magnificent exhibition *Herod the Great – The King's Final Journey* had been mounted in The Israel Museum of Jerusalem. The author greatly benefited from an early copy of the lavishly illustrated and rich catalogue. Sincere thanks are expressed here to David Mevorah, Silvia Rozenberg and Boaz Zissu for their kind assistance. In the search for illustrations, special gratitude is extended to Danny Syon for his generous help and a superb collection of coin images, and to Zeev Weiss for his expertise. The editorial work has greatly benefited from the cordial support and advice of many of our close friends, especially of Fergus Millar, Tessa Rajak, Martin Goodman and Nicholas de Lange. I am deeply indebted to Dominic Mattos from Bloomsbury and his editorial team for a friendly collaboration on the preparation of this book, and to Jonathan Kirkpatrick, Kimberley Czajkowski and Jane Barlow for giving me a helping hand. My warmest thanks go also to my son Ian for his readiness to help me at any time, day or night.

M.V.

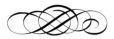

Abbreviations

Ant.	Josephus, *Jewish Antiquities*
b	*bavli* = Babylonian Talmud, followed by the name of the tractate
BAR	*Biblical Archaeology Review*
CD	Cairo *Damascus Document*
Dan	Daniel
DSD	*Dead Sea Discoveries*
Ecclus	*Ecclesiasticus* or *Wisdom of Ben Sira*
Ezek	Ezekiel
Hist.	Tacitus, *Histories*
JJS	*Journal of Jewish Studies*
Isa	Isaiah
JSOT	*Journal for the Study of the Old Testament*
Jub	Book of *Jubilees*
m	*Mishnah*, followed by the name of the tractate
Mac	Book of the *Maccabees*
Matth	Matthew
War	Josephus, *Jewish War*
4Q169	*Commentary of Nahum* from Qumran Cave 4

List of illustrations

The main events of Roman history during Herod's age

To facilitate the understanding of Herod's life and work between 73/2 and 4 BCE within international dimensions, a list of major events of Roman history, which took place during the relevant period, will be briefly set out. Readers who are interested in a fuller account may find every detail in Sir Ronald Syme's masterpiece, *The Roman Revolution*.[1]

Table of events

BCE

63	Pompey conquers Syria and Judaea
60	First triumvirate consisting of Pompey, Julius Caesar and Crassus
49	Roman civil war: Julius Caesar against Pompey
48	Caesar defeats Pompey at the battle of Pharsalus. Pompey murdered in Egypt
44	Caesar assassinated on the Ides of March
43	Second triumvirate consisting of Octavian, Mark Antony and Lepidus
42	The republicans defeated by Octavian and Antony at the battle of Philippi; Brutus and Cassius commit suicide
41–32	Antony is in the East
31	Octavian defeats Antony at the battle of Actium
30	Antony and Cleopatra commit suicide
27	Octavian is named Augustus and rules as Princeps or Emperor until 14 CE

Frontispiece *Mosaic on the floor of Herod's Mausoleum at Herodium.*

Prologue

Herod the Great, whose life and work are the subject of this book, dreamt of lifting his Jewish kingdom to a central position and of endowing it with genuine significance in the Roman Empire of Augustus. His vision continued the idealistic understanding of the role of the land of Israel and its Jewish population that we find occasionally expressed in Jewish literary sources in the second half of the pre-Christian era. The prophet Ezekiel in the mid-sixth century BCE prophesied that at the end of times the eschatological enemy, Gog of the land of Magog, would attack the peaceful Jews gathered from among the nations, who lived in the centre of the world, or as he put it, 'at the navel of the earth'.[2] The Book of Jubilees among the Pseudepigrapha, written in the mid-second century BCE, using the then prevalent Hellenistic Greek image of the earth from the Ionian world map,[3] considers Mount Zion in Jerusalem as occupying the same central position: 'Mount Zion was in the midst of the navel of the earth'.[4]

This centrality of the land of the Jews and Jerusalem is clearly displayed on medieval world maps such as the Mappa Mundi in Hereford cathedral.

Objectively judged on the level of world history, the Jews, prior to the age of Herod, never belonged to the first division or even to the second in the power game of the nations of the Near East in ancient biblical times.

The country inhabited by them was in the focal point of the opposing political aspirations of Egypt and Assyro-Babylonia, both wishing to dominate the lands lying between their respective boundaries. After the conquest of Babylon by Cyrus in 539 BCE, it fell into the hands of the new Persian world power to control the Near East. Judaea remained under the thumb of the Iranian Achaemenid kings for more than

Figure P.1 *The Hereford World Map by Richard of Haldingham and Lafford, drawn on a single sheet of vellum c. 1285* CE. *The map – as was common in the cartography of the time – shows Jerusalem at the very centre of the world.*

200 years, while these successors of Cyrus strove to establish themselves further westwards in Asia Minor and beyond, seeking to confront, without lasting success, the city-states of classical Greece.

Then at the end of the fourth century BCE, the triumphant Alexander the Great stormed across the whole Near and Middle East as far as India, and after his premature death, the Mediterranean countries were left in the hands of his Syrian and Egyptian heirs, the Seleucids and the Ptolemies. Palestine, the land of the Jews, was ruled one after the other by these two Hellenistic overlords. Then in 166/5 BCE the successful Maccabaean rebellion was launched against Antiochus IV Epiphanes, who sought forcibly to extinguish Judaism and supplant it by the Greek religion. A century-long, largely independent, Jewish state was set up by the successors of the Maccabaean brothers, known as the Hasmonaeans, who held both the religious and the secular-political reins of the nation between 152 and 63 BCE.

In 63 BCE, with Pompey the Great occupying Jerusalem, Rome took over the lead and remained the exclusive and ultimate authority until Mark Antony and Octavian persuaded the Senate to entrust the government of Judaea to the Idumaean Herod, whose ancestors were induced to adopt Judaism half a century earlier by the Hasmonaean ruling High Priest John Hyrcanus I (134–105 BCE). So before tackling in the main part of this book the life and times of Herod the Great, I will attempt to offer a fuller sketch of the development of Jewish history in the land of Israel in the course of the millennium that lead up to it, with special emphasis on the 500 years separating Cyrus from Herod.

Part One

A bird's eye view of biblical history

1

From King David to the start of the Hellenistic period

At the start of the tenth century BCE David (1010–970 BCE) and his son Solomon (970–931 BCE) reigned over a newly established independent state of small or medium importance, but after the death of Solomon, his kingdom split into Israel in the north and Judah in the south. David rebuilt the conquered Jebusite capital, Jerusalem, and Solomon enriched it with a magnificent Temple.

The principal religious innovation of the epoch that followed David and Solomon was the arrival of prophets, charismatic leaders such as Samuel and the miracle-working Elijah and Elisha. Next came the powerful preachers and spiritual guides of the eighth century BCE, the rustic Amos and the aristocratic Isaiah.

The Judaean herdsman Amos, who experienced a divine call, unhesitatingly castigated the king of Israel, Jeroboam, in the northern sanctuary of Bethel and bravely ignored the menacing words of the priest of the place, Amaziah:

O seer, go, flee away to the land of Judah, and eat bread there, and prophesy there, but never again prophesy at Bethel, for it is the king's sanctuary . . .

(Amos 7:12)

Figure 1.1 *Ruins of the city of David in Jerusalem.*

The riposte of Amos was sharp:

The Lord took me from following the flock and the Lord said to me, 'Go, prophesy to my people, Israel.'

Now therefore hear the word of the Lord.
You say, 'Do not prophesy against Israel,
And do not preach against the house of Isaac.'
Therefore thus says the Lord:
'Your wife shall be a harlot in the city,
and your sons and daughters shall fall by the sword,
and Israel must go into exile away from his land.'

(Amos 7:15–17)

In turn, in the second half of the eighth century BCE, the majestic Isaiah spoke up against routine Temple worship and advocated true internal piety:

'What to me is the multitude of your sacrifices?' says the Lord;
'I have had enough of burnt-offerings of rams
and the fat of fed beasts;
I do not delight in the blood of bulls, or of lambs, or of goats . . .
Trample my courts no more;
Bringing offerings is futile;
Incense is an abomination to me.
New moon and Sabbath and calling of convocation –
I cannot endure solemn assemblies with iniquity . . .
Wash yourselves; make yourselves clean;
Remove the evil of your doings from before my eyes;
Cease to do evil, learn to do good;
Seek justice, rescue the oppressed;
Defend the orphan, plead for the widow.'

(Isa. 1:11–17)

So did also Micah, in the eighth/seventh century, who contrasted the divinely inspired religion of the prophets with the Temple cult administered by priests:

With what shall I come before the Lord,
and bow myself before God on high?
Shall I come before him with burnt-offerings,
with calves a year old?
Will the Lord be pleased with thousands of rams,
with tens of thousands of rivers of oil?
Shall I give my firstborn for my transgression,
the fruit of my body for the sin of my soul?
He has told you, O mortal, what is good;
and what does the Lord require of you
But to do justice, and to love kindness,
and to walk humbly with your God?

(Micah 6: 6–8)

The kingdoms of Judah and Israel were threatened not only by the two great world powers, Egypt and Assyria, but even by the Philistines from the Palestinian coastal plain, and by the Aramaeans of adjacent Syria from the northern side. In 722–21 BCE the Assyrian king Shalmanezer V (727–722 BCE) conquered the Kingdom of Israel and he or his successor, Sargon II (722–705 BCE), deported many Israelites to Mesopotamia and replaced them with non-Jewish colonists (2 Kings 17:5–6). They intermarried with the remaining Jewish population, and according to the biblical account they adopted their religion, which they mixed with their ancestral paganism and thus became the Samaritans (2 Kings 17:24–41). Their place of worship was at Mount Gerizim near the city of Samaria.

The southern Kingdom of Judah managed to maintain some kind of independence for more than a century and even experienced a religious revival during the reign of King Josiah (640–609 BCE). In his days, in the course of repair works done in the Temple of Jerusalem, the High Priest reported the 'discovery' of the hidden, and thus forgotten, Book of the Law (2 Kings 22:3–10). The legend purports to sanction the reform introduced by Josiah, which was based on Deuteronomy, the fifth section of the Pentateuch, source of the so-called Deuteronomic reform. One of its principal innovations was the closing down of the previously flourishing provincial sanctuaries at Bethel, Dan, Shiloh, and so on, and their replacement by the single Temple of Jerusalem. At the start of the sixth century BCE, not heeding the warnings of the prophet Jeremiah, the independent Kingdom of Judah also came to an end. Zedekiah, the last king, rebelled against the Babylonian ruler,

Figure 1.2a *King Nebuchadnezzar on a stele he erected in Babylon. The stele shows the 'Etemenanki' (Sumerian for 'temple of the foundation of heaven and earth'). This type of raised structure is known as a Ziggurat. The representation on this stele in the Schøyen Collection, known as the 'Tower of Babel Stele' (cf. Genesis 11) is the oldest known image of the Etemenanki.*

Figure 1.2b *Line drawing of the Tower of Babel Stele, showing Nebuchadnezzar, and the great Ziggurat, more clearly.*

Nebuchadnezzar, who in 587 BCE invaded Judah and sacked Jerusalem. The Temple built by Solomon was destroyed and a substantial proportion of the Jews together with their captured and blinded king were deported to Babylonia (2 Kings 25:1–21).

The Babylonian exile, lasting slightly less than 50 years, became the turning point marking a major religious and spiritual Israelite revival, and culminating in the formulation of strict Jewish monotheism. The God of Israel was proclaimed the one and only true God and all the foreign deities were downgraded to the status of idols, under the influence of the great anonymous exilic prophet, known as the Second Isaiah (Isa. 40–55), and Ezekiel. No doubt, the priests of the tribe of Levi living in exile also guided them. Prior to this point, the Jewish religion was henotheistic – Israel worshipped only their national God just as the other peoples worshipped theirs – but from then on the Jews confessed that there was only a single and unique God: 'Hear O Israel, the Lord our God is One Lord' (Deut. 6:4).

The Second Isaiah also recognized the rising political giant, King Cyrus of Persia (559–530 BCE), as God's elect sent to restore freedom to his captive compatriots, and hailed him as his Anointed or Messiah:

Thus says the Lord to his anointed, Cyrus . . .
For the sake of my servant Jacob and Israel my chosen,

Figure 1.3a *This remarkable bas-relief shows a figure that many believe to be Cyrus the Great. It is located in Pasargadae, Iran – the capital of the Persian Empire. The horned crown is redolent of the vision in Daniel Chapter 8.*

I call you by your name,

I surname you though you do not know me.

I am the Lord, and there is no other,

Besides me there is no god.

(Isa. 45:1, 4–5)

Indeed, in the first year of his reign over Babylon and hence Jerusalem, in 539 BCE, Cyrus granted leave to the exiled Jews to return to their homeland and rebuild the Temple destroyed by the Babylonians (Ezra 1:2–4). They promptly obeyed and set out to construct a new sanctuary, more modest than that of Solomon, known as the Second

Figure 1.3b *The figure of Cyrus in a reproduction of the Pasargad relief at the Olympic Park in Sydney, Australia.*

Figure 1.4 *Persian coin. A falcon with the inscription* YHD *(Yehud), Judaea.*

Temple, and completed it between 520 and 515 BCE under the leadership of the Davidic prince Zerubbabel and the High Priest Joshua, with the wholehearted support of the prophets Haggai and Zechariah (Ezra 6:15). Half a century later, a Jewish official in the Persian court, Nehemiah, obtained permission to return to Jerusalem, and appointed governor of Judaea, he rebuilt the city and fortified its walls despite the opposition led by the governor of Samaria, Sanballat.

During the Persian period the Jews adopted Aramaic, the official language of the Empire, as their vernacular, largely replacing Hebrew. Two edicts, supposed to have been issued, the first by Cyrus and the second by Artaxerxes II (405–359 BCE), are quoted in the Book of Ezra, 6:2–5 and 7:12–26. To promote international commerce, the Persians minted special local currency, the first coins to appear in Jewish history, with the inscription *Yehud*, the Aramaic form of Judaea, and the figurative representation of a bird in blatant disregard for the Jewish religious aversion from the use of images by virtue of the second commandment of the Decalogue.

Some 50 years after the arrival in Jerusalem of Nehemiah, the priest Ezra, qualified as the Scribe or Scripture expert, returned from Babylonia in 398 BCE in the company of priests and various Temple servants, and in a solemn ceremony proclaimed the Law of Moses as the constitution of the Jewish state (Neh 8:1–8). Emphasis was laid on the strict observance of the commandments and in particular on the avoidance of mixed marriages, which were seen as a major threat to total faithfulness to the Jewish religion.

A curious but significant sidelight is shed on the Judaism of the Persian period by the Elephantine papyri, the bulk of them written in Aramaic by the Jewish soldiers of the garrison established by the Persians on the island of Jeb (Elephantine) in the fifth century BCE. They are contracts and family correspondence and matters of political importance addressed to Bagohi, the Persian governor of Judaea, and mentioning also Sanballat, the

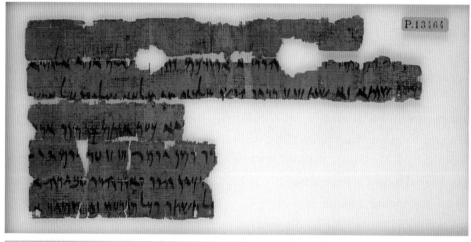

Figure 1.5 *The Passover papyrus from Elephantine, front and back. The papyrus dates to 419 BCE and was discovered in 1907.*

governor of Samaria, whose name appears also in the Book of Nehemiah (2:10, 19, etc.). One of the letters from 419 BCE sets out the rules to be observed at Passover:

Now, you thus count four[teen days in Nisan (March–April) and on the 14th at twilight ob]serve [the Passover] and from the 15th day until the 21st day of [Nisan observe the Festival of Unleavened Bread. Seven days eat unleavened bread. Now,] be pure and take heed. [Do] n[ot do] work [on the 15th day and on the 21st day of Nisan.] Do not drink [any fermented drink. And do] not [eat] anything of leaven [nor let it be seen in your houses from the 14th day of Nisan at] sunset until the 21st day of Nisa[n at sunset. And b]ring into your chambers [any leaven which you have in your houses] and seal (them) up during [these] days . . .⁵

The picture of the Elephantine Jews recalls the Jewish-Canaanite religious syncretism of the pre-exilic period. The Jeb colonists had their own temple with animal sacrifices dedicated to Yaho or Yahu (=YHWH), who had also a wife, Anath Yahu or Anath Bethel. This sanctuary was destroyed by an Egyptian mob, but a petition by the Jewish leaders of the Elephantine community to reconstruct the temple and restore the offerings of incense, vegetables and animals was not fully granted, as the permission is silent on animal sacrifices.

With the decline of prophecy after Ezra, Judaism in the Holy Land developed during the rest of the Persian period and beyond on essentially legal lines as the religion of the Torah or Mosaic Law under the control of the High Priest and the priests. By the end of the fourth century BCE the Persian hold on the Empire slackened, and repeated revolts in Phoenicia signalled the end of the age and the arrival of a new world power brought about by the meteoric rise of the Greeks under Alexander the Great.

Having defeated the last Persian ruler, at the battle of Issus in 333 BCE, by 326 BCE Alexander stretched the frontiers of his power from Greece and Egypt through the whole of the Middle East, including Judaea, as far as the Himalayas and India. Before he reached his thirty-fourth year, he was dead, suddenly struck by an illness in 323 BCE, and his Empire was divided between his generals, with Ptolemy inheriting Egypt and Seleucus the territories in Asia. During the third century BCE Judaea fluctuated between

Figure 1.6 *Alexander on a late fourth century* BCE *Hellenistic bas-relief carving on one of the sides of a great sarcophagus, now held at the Istanbul Archaeology Museum. The image shows Alexander fighting against the Persians.*

the Ptolemies and the Seleucids and was internally governed by the High Priest with his *gerousia* or council of elders.[6]

The Jews were generally left in peace as long as the High Priest paid the taxes to the Ptolemies, first in the form of a lump sum – 20 talents of silver – and later by the intermediary of Jewish tax farmers, among whom the most famous was a certain Joseph, son of Tobias, whose family, the Tobiads, played an important role in the Judaea of this age.[7] The Tobiads were the leading Jewish financiers in the third century BCE. One of them, Hyrcanus, became extremely rich and indulged in sumptuous building activities at Araq el Amir, not far from Amman in Transjordan. The remains of his palace are still visible.

The repeated changeover between Egyptian and Syrian overlords ended in 198 BCE, when the Seleucid Antiochus III the Great, victorious over Egypt at the battle of

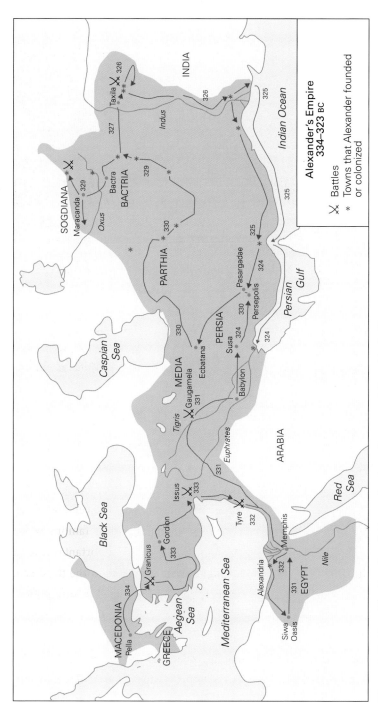

Figure 1.7 *Map: The Empire of Alexander from Greece and Egypt to India.*

Figure 1.8 *Palace of the Tobiah family at Araq el Amir near Amman. Second century* BCE. *The scale of the palace built by Hyrcanus shows the great wealth of the Tobiads.*

Figure 1.9 *Inscription of the name* Tobiah.

Paneas, north-east of Galilee, seized Judaea and attached it to the Seleucid Empire.[8] Paneas or Banias will be known as Caesarea Philippi in the New Testament.

Alexander's military conquest was followed by the progressive cultural and religious Hellenization of Egypt, Judaea, Syria and Mesopotamia under the Seleucids and the Ptolemies. The impact of Hellenism on Jewish history will be sketched in the next section.

Figure 1.10 *Antiochus III the Great (222–187 BCE). Marble head, third century BCE.*

2

From the arrival of Hellenization in Judaea to the outbreak of the Maccabaean uprising

As a natural consequence of the conquest of the Near East by Alexander the Great, the Greek language and culture, Hellenism in short, progressively spread among the nations governed by the Ptolemies and the Seleucids.[9]

'The meeting between Judaism and Hellenism is one of the most discussed relationships in cultural history', writes Tessa Rajak.[10] While internally the Jewish community of Judaea developed along the line established by Ezra, namely in faithful adherence to the Law of Moses, a line that led to the Judaism of the Mishnah and the Talmud, in real life, Hellenistic influence became unavoidable. At least a smattering of Greek was essential, not only in areas of mixed population, but simply in order to pursue foreign trade. The language, however, opened the door to culture, material culture as well as art and architecture, and to social changes and political behaviour, at least on a superficial level. So by the opening decades of the second century BCE, even before Antiochus IV Epiphanes attempted to enforce Hellenism on the people of Judaea, a significant group of upper class Jews were not only sympathetically inclined towards Hellenism, but were keen actively to promote it under the leadership of the High Priest Jason, appointed by Antiochus, against the firm opposition of the traditionalists, known as the Devout or Hasidim. This conflict is thought to be described in the Damascus Document from among the Dead Sea Scrolls as 'the age of wrath', 390 years after Nebuchadnezzar's conquest of Jerusalem, when the traitors 'departed from the way', 'transgressed the covenant and violated the precept'.[11] Amazingly, though in some way understandably, as they formed the intellectual elite of the nation, the young Jewish priests, who were expected to act as the bulwarks of the ancestral traditions, developed particular enthusiasm for cultural novelty. Instead of performing their sacred duties in the Temple, they opted for modernity and preferred to indulge in athletic exercises in the newly built sports arena.[12]

The cultural and religious crisis especially hit Judaea and Jerusalem after the accession to the Seleucid throne of Antiochus IV (175–64 BCE), surnamed Epiphanes. He was unpredictable, both generous and ferocious, and the Greek historian Polybius thought that *epimanes* (raving mad) suited him better than *epiphanes*, the god who reveals himself. He intended to turn the 'detestable' Jewish nation, to use the expression of Tacitus, into a civilized people.[13]

He was opposed by Onias III, a 'zealot for the laws',[14] but perhaps even to his own surprise, he found powerful allies at the top level of the Jerusalem society, among the members of the High Priestly families. In 174 BCE Onias's brother Jesus (Joshua), who preferred to be known under the Greek name of Jason, leader of the Hellenizing party, persuaded Antiochus to depose Onias[15] and appoint him in his stead. He then set out to turn Jerusalem into a kind of Greek city. A gymnasium (sports arena) was built, which, as has already been noted, was frequented even by the priests.[16]

Jason's ill-acquired office did not last long. In 171 BCE, a certain Menelaus, possibly not even of priestly stock, outbid him and, with the support of the influential Tobiads (Chapter 1), was given Jason's High Priesthood by Antiochus.[17] Next year, in 170 BCE, Menelaus arranged for the murder of the deposed legitimate High Priest, Onias III.[18]

While Antiochus set out to campaign in Egypt in 169 BCE, Jason attempted to regain power, thus provoking the king to organize a massacre in Jerusalem and seize all the treasure of the Temple. But the real disaster followed the second unsuccessful attack of Egypt by Antiochus IV in 168 BCE, which was halted by the ambassador of Rome who arrived with the Roman fleet. Humiliated and outraged, Antiochus sought revenge on the Jews. In 167 BCE, the inhabitants of Jerusalem were decimated by the royal envoy, Apollonius. The city and its walls were sacked and a Greek garrison was installed in the high city, the Akra. It remained in Seleucid hands for over a quarter of a century.[19]

A violent religious persecution followed. The Temple cult was abolished and the observance of the laws relating to the Sabbath and circumcision prohibited under pain of death. In December 167, a pagan altar was set up in the Temple and sacrifice was offered on it to Olympian Zeus. This was known as 'the abomination of desolation'.[20] Heroic Jews willingly sacrificed their lives for their faith in Jerusalem and in country towns,[21] but the survival of Judaism appeared to be beyond redemption.

Then something unparalleled occurred: a small people took up arms in defence of their religion and defeated the powerful oppressor. The revolution was launched by the country priest, Mattathias of Modein or Modi'in, and pursued by his five sons among whom the leading roles were played by Judas, the chief military leader, surnamed the Maccabee or Hammer, and Simon, the political brain.[22] Against all reasonable expectation, the amateur Jewish forces, joined by the group of the Devout or Hasidim, repeatedly smashed the professional armies of the Seleucid Empire at Beth-Horon, Emmaus and Beth-Zur,[23] while Antiochus himself and his main forces were busy fighting the Parthians. A disease which he contracted there killed Antiochus.

Meanwhile the triumphant Judas reoccupied Jerusalem, built a new altar in the Temple and celebrated on 25 Kislev (November/December) 164 BCE the renewed consecration of the sanctuary, followed by an eight-day-long festival known as Hanukkah[24] or Dedication,[25] thus ending the initial phase of the anti-Hellenist uprising of the Jews.

3

The Maccabee Trio:
Judas – Jonathan – Simon

For a couple of years following the restoration of Jewish worship in the Temple, Judas Maccabeus continued to strengthen his power with the positive acquiescence of Antiochus V (164–162 BCE). The persecuted Jews of Galilee and Gilead were repatriated to Judaea,[26] and Judas tried without success to recapture the Jerusalem citadel. He even routed a Seleucid expeditionary force at Beth Zacharia.[27]

However, in 162 BCE the quietly sympathetic Antiochus V was murdered by Demetrius I (162–150 BCE). He decided to reassert himself against Judas by supporting the head of the Hellenizing party, the new High Priest Alcimus. Surprisingly, he was also recognized by the devout Hasidim, at the other end of the political spectrum.[28] This preferment of Alcimus to himself persuaded Onias IV, son or nephew of the murdered Onias III, to give up the fight for the pontifical succession and emigrate with a group of his followers to Egypt.[29] They were permitted to settle by Ptolemy Philometor at Leontopolis in the district of Heliopolis and, like their predecessors on the island of Jeb-Elephantine, they built a Jewish Temple, modelled on that of Jerusalem, where sacrificial worship was performed. Onias no doubt saw the justification of this innovation in a prophecy of Isaiah, foretelling Jewish settlements in five Egyptian cities and the building of an altar there.[30] This sanctuary at Leontopolis survived until the first century CE and was destroyed by the Romans, three years after the Jerusalem Temple, in 73 CE.[31]

Another army was sent to Judaea by the Seleucid ruler Demetrius, commanded by Nicanor, but he was utterly overpowered by the Jewish forces at Adasa on

'Nicanor's day' in the spring of 161 BCE.[32] In a shrewd diplomatic move to strengthen his position, Judas followed up his victory by concluding a treaty of friendship with Rome.[33]

However, the glory days with legendary 'signs and wonders' were not to last. Demetrius I was determined to bring to heel the recalcitrant Judas and sent his leading general Bacchides to implement his policy. At Elasa, the Jewish fighters were annihilated, Judas among them. His brothers, Jonathan and Simon, retrieved his body and buried him in Modi'in in the family tomb, while the people mournfully sang: 'How is the mighty fallen, the saviour of Israel!'[34]

This outcome was inevitable; the improvised and inexpert Jewish state had no chance to overcome in open warfare the united power of the Seleucid Empire.

Jonathan, Judas's younger brother, took over the leadership in 161 BCE. The pro-Greek High Priest, Alcimus, died in the following year and neither the Books of the Maccabees nor Josephus report that he was replaced. From 160 to 153 BCE the pontifical office remained vacant. These are indeed seven dark years about which our sources contain no information.

International politics affecting Judaea reawakened in 153 BCE when a Syrian court official, Alexander Balas, set out to oust Demetrius I and successfully proclaim himself king (150–145 BCE). To gain Jonathan's support, he recognized him as High Priest and military ruler (*strategos*) of Judaea.[35] A few years later Demetrius II (145–140 BCE) ousted Alexander, but Alexander's son Antiochus was backed by Tryphon, a former general of his father, and by Jonathan. Jonathan sought to gain further importance by renewing the alliance with Rome, which was first established by Judas.[36] The wily Tryphon tried to get the better of him; he persuaded Jonathan to visit Ptolemais with a small bodyguard, captured him there and later arranged for his murder.[37] Simon buried Jonathan in Modi'in and replaced him as head of state.[38]

In regard to religious politics, dealing with the leadership of Jonathan, Josephus mentions in passing the existence of three famous Jewish 'sects' or religious parties, the Pharisees, the Sadducees and the Essenes:

The Pharisees ... say that certain events are the work of Fate (i.e. Providence) ... as to other events, it depends on ourselves ... The sect of the Essenes ... declares that Fate is mistress of all things ... The Sadducees do away with Fate, holding ... that all human actions ... lie within our power ...[39]

Simon was the third Maccabee brother to hold the two chief offices of state, the High Priesthood and the political leadership of the Jews. Meanwhile Tryphon managed to climb on the Seleucid throne and endeavoured to placate Simon by exempting him from taxes and permitting him to issue his own coinage.[40] In June 141, Simon occupied the Akra, the citadel of Jerusalem, which neither of his older brothers had managed to do. A new chronological era was introduced in 143 BCE, referring to the 'First year of Simon, the great High Priest and Commander and Leader of the Jews'.[41] Indeed, in 140 BCE, an assembly of priests and lay Jews decreed that Simon 'should be their leader and High Priest *for ever*', or more precisely 'until a trustworthy prophet should arise' to express a different divine decision.[42] The decision was engraved on bronze tablets and was deposited in the Temple with copies in the Treasury,[43] thus imitating, as Tessa Rajak remarks, the usage of the Greek city.[44] Thus Simon launched the hereditary dynasty known as that of the Hasmonaeans, named after *Hasmon* or *Hasmonaios*, the great-grandfather of the Maccabee patriarch, Mattathias.[45]

Like all his brothers, Simon also experienced violent death but his was less heroic than theirs. He did not fall in fighting nor was he murdered by a Gentile enemy, but while he was in a drunken stupor, he was ingloriously assassinated together with two of his sons in the fortress of Dok by his son-in-law, Ptolemy, the son of Abubus, governor of the Jericho area, who wished to supplant him as leader of Judaea.[46]

4

The Hasmonaeans from John Hyrcanus to Mattathias Antigonus

John (Yohanan) Hyrcanus I (135–104 BCE)

John, surnamed Hyrcanus, the last surviving son of Simon Maccabeus, took over the leadership from his assassinated father. Despite their claim of being the defenders of Jewish identity and independence, they allowed Hellenism to creep in one way or another. Among other things, they all bore both Jewish and Greek names.[47]

The first six years of John were affected by the struggle to keep himself independent from foreign power during the successive Seleucid kings, Antiochus VII, Alexander Zebinas, Antiochus VIII and Antiochus IX, but by 129 BCE the Syrian supremacy came to an end. In consequence, Hyrcanus I felt free to extend his dominion. His chief conquest was the district of Samaria, entailing the sacking of the capital city. According to a Jewish legend, recorded by Josephus and the rabbis, while offering incense in the Temple, the High Priest saw in a prophetic vision the victory of his army.[48] He seized also Scythopolis, the biblical city of Beth She'an, south of the Lake of Galilee.[49]

A major political change resulted from Hyrcanus's jilting of the Pharisees, who previously controlled the interpretation and administration of the Mosaic Law. Indeed, this former pupil of the Pharisees[50] attached himself to the High Priestly Sadducees and their aristocratic supporters. Many of these used to belong to the pro-Greek party, and without ignoring the religious law, they were also committed to matters of this world.

Yet another Jewish legend, echoed by Josephus, attributes the break with the Pharisees to the unwise suggestion made by Eleazar, one of their leaders. He proposed that John should resign as High Priest and be content with being the political head of the Jewish community. He renewed the gossip that John was disqualified from holding the High Priesthood because his mother had been held captive under Antiochus Epiphanes. Outraged by this groundless charge, Hyrcanus was further infuriated when the Pharisees failed to condemn Eleazar to death for calumniously insulting the High Priest. They were all declared *personae non gratae* and it was then that John Hyrcanus became a Sadducee.[51]

Whether John Hyrcanus I minted his own coins was for a long time a subject of debate. He probably issued some inscribed only with his Hebrew name, Yohanan. The majority of coins carrying the inscription 'Yohanan the High Priest and the congregation (*hever*) of the Jews' almost certainly belong to John Hyrcanus II.

Although John used only the High Priestly title on the coins attributed to him, the very fact that he issued his own currency indicates that he wished to be seen as a Prince,

Figure 4.1 *A Yohanan (John Hyrcanus) coin obverse and reverse.*

albeit one who ruled in association with a national assembly, the congregation of the Jews.

Josephus solemnly proclaims that Hyrcanus I attained the summit of political and religious achievements, the leadership of the people, the pontificate and the prophetic status.[52] This is indirectly matched by a tradition preserved in the Aramaic Targum of Pseudo-Jonathan in Deuteronomy 33:11, where he is compared to the great prophet Elijah and a solemn curse is put on all his opponents: 'As for the enemies of John the High Priest, may they have no foot to stand on'.[53]

Finally, it should be reported that the conquest by Hyrcanus I of Idumaea was followed by the voluntary Judaization of the inhabitants, circumcision and adoption of the Jewish customs. The Idumaean Antipas or Antipater, Herod's grandfather, was appointed governor of the province.[54] His promotion constitutes the first join between Hasmonaean history and that of Herod the Great.[55] From the time of John Hyrcanus I, the Idumaeans counted as Jews although, as we shall see, some of Herod's critics could not quite stomach this idea.[56]

Judah (Yehudah) Aristobulus I (104–103 BCE)

If Josephus is correct, the heir of John Hyrcanus I, Aristobulus I (104–103 BCE), having also the Jewish name of Judas,[57] was the first Hasmonaean ruler to use the royal title, but neither this title nor his Greek name appears on the coins which are ascribed to him by numismatists. Josephus paints a gruesome picture of the accession of Aristobulus. He is said to have allowed his mother, who inherited the ruling power from his father, to starve in prison, and also killed one of his brothers and put the three others behind bars.[58] By contrast, the Greek historians (Strabo following Timagenes) depict him as a 'kindly person' and a 'benefactor of the Jews'.[59] The negative version is sometimes attributed to calumny spread by Aristobulus's political adversaries.

His most notable accomplishment during his short government was the extension of the Jewish territory towards the north by the conquest of Ituraea and the enforced Judaization of the inhabitants, who were compelled to undergo circumcision and accept life under Jewish law if they wanted to avoid what we now call ethnic cleansing.[60]

Figure 4.2 *Coin of Judah (Aristobulus) obverse and reverse.*

It is debated whether the Yehudah (Judas) coins were issued by Aristobulus I or Aristobulus II (67–63 BCE). These bronze units display only the Hebrew name Yehudah and despite Josephus's assertion that Aristobulus considered himself king, refer only to his priestly function: 'Yehudah the High Priest and the congregation of the Jews'.

Alexander Jannaeus (Yehonathan) (103–76 BCE)

Aristobulus I's brief rule was followed for the next twenty-seven years by that of Alexander Jannaeus (103–76 BCE). Jannaeus, or the shortened Hebrew form, Yannai, stands for Jonathan as his currency makes plain. Jannaeus was released from jail by the widow of John Hyrcanus, Salina Alexandra, Salina standing for Salome, who became his wife and later his successor.[61] Jannaeus was the most bellicose of all the Hasmonaeans. The beginning of his rule entailed skirmishes with the Egyptian king, Ptolemy Lathyrus, but by the mid-90s BCE Jannaeus was free to attack the neighbouring territories, especially the Mediterranean coastal region, and seized the cities of Raphia, Anthedon and Gaza.[62] He later added to the considerably enlarged Jewish territory east of the Jordan the Greek cities of Pella, Gerasa and Gamala, whose continued survival was made dependent on their adoption of the customs of the Jews.[63]

Yet at home all was not well and civil unrest continued for six years. In disfavour, the Pharisees plotted the downfall of Jannaeus. Josephus reports that on one occasion they

Figure 4.3 *Coin: Yehonathan the High Priest and the congregation of the Jews (Hebrew).*

pelted him with citrons, while he was officiating in the Temple at the feast of Tabernacles, and the mayhem resulted in a massacre.[64] To get the better of him, in 88 BCE the Pharisees persuaded the Seleucid Demetrius III to invade Judaea. He defeated Jannaeus's army of mercenaries and returned to Syria.[65] Jannaeus managed to escape and sought revenge, capturing many antagonistic Pharisees and cruelly executing 800 of them by crucifixion.[66]

Alexander Jannaeus was the first Hasmonaean ruler emphatically to proclaim his royal status. The term 'King' appears on his coins, some of which are bilingual, either Hebrew and Greek or Aramaic and Greek. Some of the currency struck by him carries the already traditional formula, 'Yehonathan (or Yonathan) the High Priest and the congregation of the Jews', but we have also the Hebrew 'Yehonathan the King', accompanied by the Greek 'King Alexander' and on the Aramaic-Greek specimen, minted in 78 BCE, the Hebrew name is altogether omitted with the legend simply giving 'King Alexander'.[67] His many political and military exertions, combined with heavy drinking, brought Jannaeus prematurely to the grave at the age of 49 years, in 76 BCE.

Salome (Shelamzion) Alexandra (76–67 BCE)

On his deathbed Alexander Jannaeus left the royal power to his wife, Salome-Salina, surnamed Alexandra (76–67 BCE), and she appointed her eldest son, John Hyrcanus, to

Figure 4.4 *Coin: King Alexander (Greek) –*
Yehonathan the King (Hebrew).

the pontifical office.[68] The queen was also enjoined by her husband to make peace with
the Pharisees, too influential to be left in the background: 'Promise them ... that you
will not take any action ... on the throne without their consent.'[69] Return into favour
encouraged the Pharisees to seek revenge on the dead king's (Sadducee) advisers
responsible for the crucifixion of the 800 Pharisees, but the (Sadducee) opposition was
still influential enough to prevent the royal consent.[70] By contrast, it has been surmised
that the rabbinic story of the 'hanging' (or crucifixion) by the Pharisee leader Simeon
ben Shetah of eighty witches in Ascalon[71] is a veiled reference to the revenge execution
of Sadducees in the reign of Alexandra.[72]

The pious and God-fearing queen died at the age of 73 years, expecting to be
succeeded by Hyrcanus II, but his younger brother, the ambitious and dynamic
Aristobulus, was ready to raise the flag of rebellion leading to a four-year-long civil war.

Figure 4.5 *Map of the Maccabaean-Hasmonaean Jewish state.*

Legend:
- Jewish state under Judas
- Additions under Jonathan
- Additions under Simon
- Additions under John Hyrcanus
- Additions under Aristobulus I
- Additions under Alexander Jannaeus

Sidon

Tyre

Paneas

Gischala

Ptolemais

Lake of Galilee

Gamala

Hippos

Mediterranean Sea

Sepphoris

Gadara

Dora

Megiddo

Arbela

Strato's Tower

Scythopolis

Pella

Samaria

Jordan

Gerasa

Apollonia

Joppa

Gilgal

Timnath

Philadelphia

Lydda

Modein   Beth-Horon

Jamnia   Gezer

Adasa   Jericho

Heshbon

Azotus

Jerusalem

Madaba

Ascalon

Marisa   Beth-Zur

Anthedon

Lachish   Hebron

Machaerus

Gaza

Dead Sea

Raphia

Masada

Beersheba

Rabbath Moab

0   10   20   30 m

0   15   30   45 km

Judas (Yehudah) Aristobulus II (67–63 BCE)

On the death of their mother, Salome Alexandra, war broke out between the legitimate heir, John Hyrcanus, and his younger brother, Judas Aristobulus. Aristobulus gained the upper hand at the battle fought at Jericho. Hyrcanus withdrew to Jerusalem and ceded the kingly and High Priestly titles to Aristobulus.[73] The influential Idumaean leader Antipater, Herod's father, gave his support to the weak Hyrcanus, who appeared easier to manipulate, and obtained for him refuge in Petra with the Nabataeans. Their king Aretas, after defeating Aristobulus, besieged him at the Temple Mount in Jerusalem.[74]

Meanwhile Pompey, the Roman conqueror of Syria, sent one of his generals, Marcus Aemilius Scaurus, to Damascus in 65 BCE. Scaurus, learning about the civil conflict between Hyrcanus and Aristobulus, travelled at once to Jerusalem, sided with the more energetic Aristobulus, and first chased then overpowered Aretas.[75] He celebrated this victory on one of his coins inscribed M. Scaurus, with a kneeling and thus surrendering King (*Rex*) Aretas depicted there next to a Nabataean camel.

On Pompey's arrival in Damascus in 63 BCE, he was approached by Jewish delegations sent by the two brothers.[76] Pompey dispatched Gabinius to take Jerusalem, but since Aristobulus's supporters resisted, he returned to Pompey who, furious, arrested

Figure 4.6 *Coin of Scaurus with the surrendering King Aretas.*

Aristobulus.[77] Pompey then entered Jerusalem without a fight, but on the Temple Mount the Jewish forces refused to surrender and a three-month-long siege followed, ending with Roman victory on the Day of Atonement 63 BCE.[78] Pompey, curious, entered the Holy of Holies of the Temple, left it intact, and ordered the regular worship to continue.[79] He seized the coastal towns, as well as Samaria, Scythopolis and the cities of Transjordan conquered by Janneaus.[80] John Hyrcanus II was allowed to act as High Priest, but was deprived of the royal title. At his triumph in Rome, celebrated in 61 BCE, the former Jewish priestly ruler Aristobulus II was obliged to walk in front of the victor's chariot. He was released from jail by Julius Caesar after he had ousted Pompey from power, but at the end Aristobulus perished, poisoned in 49 BCE by Pompey's adherents.[81]

More than two millennia were to pass from the Roman conquest of Jerusalem in 63 BCE until 1948, when the new independent Jewish state of Israel was created by the United Nations.

John (Yehohanan) Hyrcanus II (63–40 BCE)

Hyrcanus's history, like that of Antipater and his son Herod, is completely tied up with the Roman civil wars between Pompey and Julius Caesar, Caesar's murderers, Brutus and Cassius, and Mark Antony and Octavian, finally between Antony and Octavian, the great-nephew and heir of Caesar. Both Hyrcanus and Antipater endeared themselves to Caesar, the former persuading the Egyptian Jews to support Caesar, and the latter giving military aid to his troops at Alexandria. To reward them, Caesar confirmed Hyrcanus's status as High Priest and hereditary ethnarch, and returned to him the port of Joppa (Jaffa) and other cities removed by Pompey from Jewish jurisdiction. As for Antipater, he was granted Roman citizenship and exemption from taxes and was named procurator of Judaea.[82] The Jews of Alexandria and Asia Minor also benefitted from Caesar's goodwill.[83] Not surprisingly his violent passing on 15 March 44 BCE was deeply mourned by Rome's Jewish community:

Public grief was enhanced by crowds of foreigners lamenting in their own fashions, *especially Jews*, who came flocking to the Forum for several nights in succession.[84]

Figure 4.7 *Coin of John Hyrcanus II.*

After Caesar's murder the fate of the leaders of Judaea, Hyrcanus as well as Antipater and Herod, depended on the provisional master of Syria, one of the murderous 'liberators', Gaius Cassius Longinus, to whom they all submitted themselves.[85] By then Antipater was no longer alive, having been poisoned in 43 BCE by Hyrcanus's butler at the instigation of Malichus.[86]

The invasion of Judaea by the Parthians in 40 BCE was the next catastrophe that hit Hyrcanus. His nephew, Mattathias Antigonus, the son of Aristobulus II, was made the puppet king of Judaea by the Parthians.[87] Hyrcanus and Phasael, Herod's brother, were handed over to him, but Herod managed to escape from Jerusalem to Petra in Nabataea.[88] Antigonus saw to it that Hyrcanus would never regain the High Priesthood: he cut or bit off one of his ears, and thus made him unfit for the office according to Jewish law.[89] The imprisoned Phasael committed suicide by dashing his head against a rock and Hyrcanus was taken to Parthia as a prisoner.[90] With the passing of both his father Antipater, and his elder brother, Phasael, Herod became the head of the family.

Mattathiah (Mattathias) Antigonus (40–37 BCE)

The end period of the Hasmonaeans coincided with the Roman takeover of Judaea from the Parthians and their Jewish ruler, Antigonus, for the benefit of Herod. Perhaps the weakest of the Hasmonaean line, Mattathias Antigonus imitated Alexander Jannaeus

Figure 4.8 *Coin of Mattathias Antigonus. Obverse in Hebrew: Mattathiah the High Priest; reverse in Greek: King Antigonus.*

in designating himself as king on the Greek legend of his currency, but his ephemeral kingship marked the end of the Hasmonaean rule.

Having been appointed king by the Senate on the recommendation of Mark Antony and Octavian in 40 BCE,[91] Herod sailed to Ptolemais in the following year.[92] He overcame Antigonus's forces whose general, Pappus, fell on the battlefield.[93] The siege of the capital followed in 37 BCE with the powerful assistance of the governor of Syria, Sosius.

King Antigonus gave himself up to the Roman general, who humiliated him by calling him Antigone as though he were a woman.[94] He was taken to Antioch on Herod's request and by Mark Antony's order he was decapitated. He was the first king defeated by the Romans to suffer such a disgrace.[95]

Part Two

Herod the Great

Introduction

Herod the Great was an outstanding figure in the history of his age as a statesman, a champion of culture and the creator of architectural masterpieces, yet Western civilization has inherited a wholly negative image of the king during whose reign Jesus of Nazareth was born.[96] The legendary account of Matthew in the first two chapters of his Gospel, ancient and modern Nativity plays and Christian imagination have turned Herod into the Ivan the Terrible of antiquity. When the three wise kings of Christian tradition, that is the Zoroastrian priests or oriental magicians (*magoi*) of the Greek Gospel, arrived at the royal palace in Jerusalem and inquired about the recently born Jewish prince, Herod pretended to be helpful, consulted the Jewish chief priests, his biblical experts, and on condition that the visitors would let him know the precise whereabouts of the babe, he directed them to Bethlehem, the traditional birthplace of the Messiah, following the prediction of the prophet Micah:

And you, O Bethlehem, in the land of Judah, are by no means least among the rulers of Judah; for from you shall come a ruler who will govern my people Israel.[97]

He himself also wished to greet the babe, Herod lied, when in fact he planned to murder any potential rival. So when the magi, warned in a dream in the Matthean legend, failed to return to Jerusalem, Herod let loose his soldiers, who massacred the infants of Bethlehem under the age of two, except the one the king dreaded. In turn, the Gospel of Luke supplies a different Herodian connection. According to this, Herod was the ruler of Judaea in whose days took place a Roman world census that compelled Joseph and Mary to travel from Nazareth in Galilee to Bethlehem in Judaea.[98]

Both birth stories are fictional or twisted. The killing of the innocents is probably a legend, patterned on Pharaoh's decree against Jewish baby boys in the age of Moses at the time of the Exodus from Egypt.[99] As for the census, whose purpose was to prepare the introduction of Roman taxation in Judaea, it could not have occurred during Herod's reign. As a friend of Rome, a *rex socius* or allied king, he was exempt from such interference.[100] There was indeed a real property census conducted, as Luke states, by Quirinius, governor of Syria, but that happened in 6 CE, ten years after Herod's death. It was then that Judaea became a Roman province directly administered by a governor sent by Augustus.[101]

The tax registration caused a political storm and brought about the birth of the Jewish revolutionary party of the *Sicarii* or Zealots.[102] Established by two revolutionary leaders, Judas the Galilean, called also Judas of Gamala, and the Pharisee Zadok, the members of this movement were mostly responsible for all the rebellious activities which characterized Judaean history throughout the first century CE up to, and especially during, the first war against Rome (66–70 CE), and even beyond, till the fall of their last stronghold, Masada, and their mass suicide in 74 CE.[103]

The real Herod figures prominently in both Jewish and Roman history too, and his biography is recorded in every particular.[104] As the renowned Josephus expert L. H. Feldman notes, 'There is no figure in antiquity about whom we have more detailed information than Herod'.[105] In addition, rabbis in the Talmud and Midrash occasionally quote Jewish anecdotes relating to Herod's life and time, some linked to his reconstruction of the Jerusalem Temple or to his favourite breed of domesticated pigeons, known under the name of Herodian doves.[106]

Our chief informant regarding Herod's life and times is the already mentioned Flavius Josephus (37–c. 100 CE), a Jewish priest, statesman and writer, four of whose works, the *Jewish War*, the *Jewish Antiquities*, his *Life* and an apology of Judaism, entitled *Against Apion*, have survived.[107] Unfortunately we have no contemporary, or near-contemporary, representation of Josephus and the earliest available document is an amusing drawing contained in a ninth-century manuscript, sketching him as a Jewish priest as imagined by the anonymous artist.[108]

Flavius Josephus consecrated to Herod's imposing figure most of Book I of the *Jewish War*, written in the late seventies, and Books XIV–XVII of the *Jewish Antiquities*, completed in the nineties of the first century CE. Josephus, who was born about forty years after the death of Herod, had good access to sources regarding the history of the Herodian age. His principal source was the *Universal History* of Nicolas of Damascus, a learned Greek philosopher and diplomat, who, after tutoring the children of Antony and Cleopatra in Egypt, joined before 14 BCE the Herodian establishment as a court official.[109] He recorded the chronicle of the reign and acted also as the king's adviser, teacher and ambassador.

Nicolas was not an objective historian; as a courtier, he sought first and foremost to please his master. His bias is particularly obvious when he wrongly presents the execution of Herod's beloved wife Mariamme and of her two sons as just punishment for her unfaithfulness and the sons' treachery. In fact, all three were innocent. Josephus makes strenuous efforts to ensure, no doubt relying on another pro-Hasmonaean source, that his readers are not misled. To further highlight the reliability of his own account, he boasts that, being himself of Jewish royal and priestly stock – one of his ancestors having married the daughter of the Jewish Hasmonaean priest-king, Alexander Jannaeus[110] – a lie would never pass his lips. His love of veracity, he claims, exceeds even his respect for the surviving members of the Herodian dynasty. He had in mind in particular King Agrippa II, whose displeasure was bound to be provoked by Josephus's not infrequent critical remarks about the family's honoured ancestor. Josephus's statement deserves to be quoted verbatim:

[Nicolas] lived during Herod's reign, as an associate of the king, and therefore wrote to please him and be of service to him, while excusing or resolutely concealing his notorious injustices. The deaths of Mariamme and her sons, for example, were acts of the grossest cruelty on the king's part, but Nicolas, wishing to present them in a good light, falsely accuses her of sexual misconduct and the young men of treachery. He remains consistent throughout his work, heaping fulsome praise upon the king's just dealings while doing his best to defend his unlawful acts . . . We, however, who belong to a family closely related to the Hasmonaean kings which has the priesthood among its honours, consider it improper to tell lies about them [Herod and his successors] and offer an honest and fair account of their doings. Many descendants of that line are still in power, and while we respect them we honour the truth even more. Indeed, there have been occasions when fair comment has incurred their anger.[111]

In addition to the work of Nicolas, Josephus must also have had at his disposal an account critical of Herod, which negatively recounts his conflict with the Hasmonaean family. These heirs of the Maccabees championed Jewish religious and political independence from 152 BCE to the Roman conquest of Judaea in 63 BCE. Josephus alludes furthermore to a work called Herod's Memoirs,[112] but without claiming to have had proper access to it. Moreover, he once refers to a Jewish popular tradition, mentioned also in the Babylonian Talmud, according to which, during all the years of the reconstruction of the Temple, it never rained in daytime so as not to slow down the work of the builders.[113]

In modern parlance Herod is regularly called 'the Great', but this honorific title is not very often applied to him in the ancient sources. Josephus uses the epithet *ho megas* (the Great) three times in connection with King Herod.[114] It has been suggested that Josephus's aim was to differentiate him from his less distinguished later descendants such as Herod Antipas or Herod Agrippa, both also mentioned in the New Testament.[115] But this argument is far from convincing as at least once he calls the less significant Agrippa I a 'great king'.[116] Also, as the author of the latest life of Herod, Ernst Baltrusch, notes, the fact that Josephus has devoted to Herod one fifth of his history from the creation to his own time reveals the importance he granted to the ruler with the epithet, 'the Great'.[117]

5

Herod prior to his appointment as king (73/2–40 BCE)

What do we know about King Herod's background? Herod came from a leading Idumaean family. The Idumaeans or Edomites were the native inhabitants of southern Palestine. His grandfather, Antipas, was appointed governor of Idumaea during the reign of the Jewish Hasmonaean High Priest, John Hyrcanus I (see Chapter 4). His father, Antipater, married Cypros, a girl who came from an illustrious Nabataean family. The Nabataeans were an Arab tribe settled in southern Jordan and spoke an Aramaic dialect. Antipater and Cypros had five children: Phasael, Herod, Joseph, Pheroras and a daughter called Salome.[118] The parents and Herod bore Greek names, their other children, male and female, were given Semitic ones. As Herod was 25 years old in 47 BCE, he must have been born in 73 or 72. He was pushing 70 when he died in the spring of 4 BCE, shortly before Passover.[119]

Since his Idumaean forebears were converted to Judaism by the Jewish High Priest John Hyrcanus,[120] Herod legally counted as a Jew, although in the eyes of his rival, the Hasmonaean prince Mattathias Antigonus, royal High Priest from 40 to 37 BCE, this Idumaean upstart was unfit to occupy the throne of Judaea as he was only a 'half-Jew' (*hemi-Ioudaios*).[121] By contrast, Nicolas of Damascus, no doubt to gratify Herod, invented for him a phony pedigree. He described Herod as the progeny of distinguished Jews repatriated to Judaea after the Babylonian exile in the second half of the sixth century BCE.[122]

As will be shown further on, when in the Holy Land, Herod acted as a Jew and strictly observed the laws of the Torah. His reconstruction of the Temple out of his own pocket must also have been motivated by his attachment to, and appreciation of, Judaism.[123] No doubt on account of his respect for Jewish opposition to the representation of human figures, he did not allow any statue of his to be set up in the Jewish territories. Neither did he authorize the impression of his effigy or that of the Emperor on his coins, contenting himself with innocuous decorative motifs, palm branches, cornucopiae, tripods and the like. His later descendants, such as his grandson Agrippa I (37–44 CE) and great-grandson Agrippa II (50–c. 92/3 CE), were less shy and allowed their portraits to decorate their coinage.

Figure 5.1 *Coin of Herod the King.*

In the opinion of archaeologists, some of the pools discovered in the Herodian palaces were intended for ritual purification. Herod's observance of the Mosaic dietary laws was also proverbial in the Roman world, and a Latin poet, Persius, even designated the Jewish Sabbath as 'Herod's day'.[124] He strictly adhered to the Mosaic legislation governing mixed marriages and required circumcision of non-Jewish men before they were allowed to marry into his family. If they refused, the engagement was called off.

It is sheer bad luck that not a single statue of Herod has survived despite the large number of his building enterprises beyond the frontiers of Palestine. The closest we came to a statue of his was in the ruins of a Nabataean temple of Baal Shamin at Si'a, south of Damascus, where a pedestal of a life size statue was found with only a foot remaining on it. The Greek inscription on the pedestal proves that the sculpture it once carried was that of King Herod. Unfortunately the statue attached to the pedestal had long since disappeared, and later on even the pedestal vanished. Luckily, however, the Greek epigraph was copied by W. H. Waddington, the French epigraphist of English stock, who at one time was prime minister of France, and it was published in *Orientis Graeci Inscriptiones Selectae*:[125]

[βα]σιλεῖ Ἡρῴδει κυρίῳ Οβαισατος Σαοδου ἔθηκε τὸν ἀνδριάντα ταῖς ἐμαῖς δαπάναι[ς] (OGIS 415)

'To King Herod, Master, I, Obaisath son of Saodos erected the statue at my own expense'.

Herod's father, Antipater, was a devoted and faithful political adviser and chief financial administrator of the Hasmonaean High Priest Hyrcanus II (63–40 BCE), first under Pompey, who conquered Judaea for Rome in 63 BCE, and later under Julius Caesar after Pompey was defeated by him at Pharsalus in 48 BCE.[126]

Antipater was an excellent soldier who often distinguished himself in combat. Josephus notes that on one occasion he stripped off his tunic in the presence of Julius Caesar to display the many battle scars he had earned in the service of Rome.[127] As a reward for his assistance to Caesar in Egypt, he was exempted from taxes and was granted Roman citizenship,[128] an honour that was bestowed on Herod too. Antipater was moreover procurator (*epitropos*, financial administrator) of Judaea.[129] After Julius Caesar's bloody demise on the Ides of March in 44 BCE, Antipater found himself willy-nilly under the authority of Cassius, one of Caesar's murderers, who took charge of Syria.[130] The following year his life came to an end. His enemy, Malichus bribed the butler of Hyrcanus to poison him. Herod, the devoted son, saw to it that Malichus would pay with his life for his crime.[131]

THE MACCABEES AND THE HASMONAEANS (166 BC–AD 100)

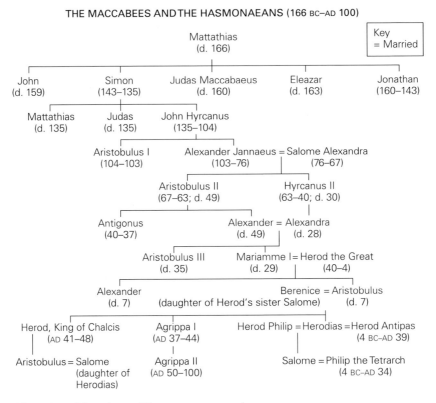

Figure 5.2 *Maccabaean/Hasmonaean genealogy.*

Josephus makes no allusion to Herod's childhood. From the Greek names of both his grandfather and his father, and from the Hellenistic inclination he exhibited in later life, it is reasonable to deduce that the young man was subjected to a Greek upbringing, which entailed the skills of reading and writing in Greek, physical and musical training, and the study of Homer, primarily the Iliad and with it Greek mythology. Remarkably, Herod's classical education continued even late in life thanks to the influence of the already mentioned Nicolas of Damascus, who had joined his court by 14 BC when Herod was nearing 60. In a surviving passage of his autobiography, Nicolas records that Herod's first enthusiasm was for philosophy. Then he was attracted to rhetoric, the art of debating, which he practised with his teacher. Next he fell in love with history and

Figure 5.3 *Bust of Julius Caesar, Vatican Museum, Rome.*

steadily pressed Nicolas to complete his *Universal History*. Finally, when he sailed to Rome to meet Augustus in 12 BCE, he took Nicolas with him to fill the empty hours of the long journey with philosophical discussions.[132]

Herod was 25 years old when Josephus first mentions him as governor of Galilee, appointed by his father in 47 BCE. The three Idumaeans, Antipater, Herod and his elder brother Phasael, governor of Judaea, exercised quasi-royal powers in the land with the agreement of the ineffectual and accommodating Hasmonaean High Priest Hyrcanus II, who ruled only in name.[133]

The dominant, indeed ruthless, character of Herod revealed itself at an early stage. In an operation intended to rid the Galilean territory of marauding brigands, he caught many of them including their leader, Ezechias, and without further ado put all of them to the sword. Herod's military success provoked the jealousy of the courtiers of Hyrcanus. They prevailed on the High Priest, aided and abetted by the crying mothers of the murdered Galileans, to indict Herod before the supreme tribunal on the charge of executing people without the due process of law. Herod was not frightened. Instead of appearing humble and repentant and showing respect to the court, he turned up clothed in purple and brought with him a strong bodyguard. The combined intervention of the Roman governor of Syria, Sextus Caesar, and the High Priest Hyrcanus II ensured his prompt acquittal. Sextus Caesar also appointed him governor of Coele-Syria, comprising parts of Syria, Lebanon, Samaria and Transjordan.[134] Josephus records that one of the judges, a Pharisee, named Samaias in the *Jewish War* and Pollio in the *Antiquities*, bravely criticized Herod and correctly foretold that one day he would repay the judges. Indeed, immediately on becoming king, Herod avenged himself on the members of the court. However, he exempted Samaias or Pollio, whose courage and integrity he admired, and whose *persona grata* status was further improved when in 37 BCE he persuaded the inhabitants of Jerusalem to welcome Herod as their new ruler.[135] His liking for the Pharisees found renewed expression when, on account of the same Samaias or Pollio, he excused the members of the group from the oath of allegiance that he had imposed on all his Jewish subjects.[136] The same privilege was also extended onto the community of the Essenes as a sign of appreciation for the prediction given by the sect's prophet Menahem to the young Herod. With a gentle tap

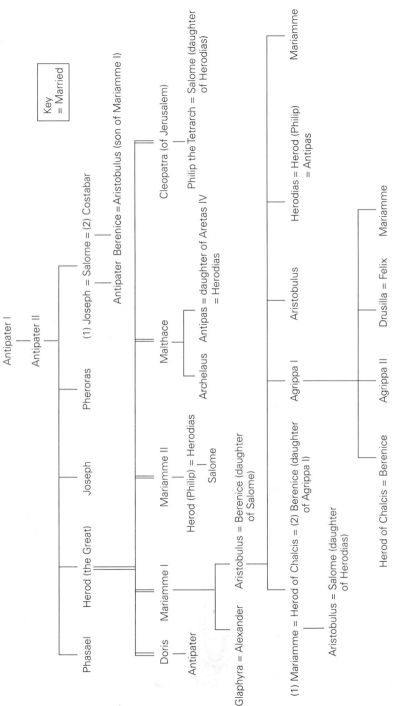

Figure 5.4 *Herodian family tree.*

on the boy's buttock, this Menahem announced that one day he would become king.[137] Herod could be friendly, appreciative and generous as well as ferocious and vengeful.

The first period of Herod's public career faithfully reflects the toing and froing of the power struggle in Rome. He and his father were always shrewd as well as lucky, and they unfailingly chose the victor's side. They first supported Pompey, conqueror of Judaea and Jerusalem in 63 BCE, but conveniently changed their allegiance to Caesar after his victory over Pompey at Pharsalus in 48 BCE. Antipater with his 3,000 soldiers helped Caesar's cause in Egypt.[138] When Cassius, one of Caesar's murderers, took over Syria in 43 BCE, Herod hastened to declare himself his devoted ally and was rewarded again by the governorship of Coele-Syria.[139] However, after the victory of Octavian and Mark Antony over Brutus and Cassius at Philippi in 42 BCE, Herod managed once more

Figure 5.5 *Bust of Mark Antony, Centrale Montemartini, Rome.*

smoothly to switch loyalty, and with the help of a large bribe, he gained the favour of Mark Antony, who became the plenipotentiary of Rome in the east. In 41 BCE, Antony appointed Herod and his brother Phasael tetrarchs, joint rulers of Judaea.[140]

In the following year, 40 BCE, Judaea was invaded by the Parthians, the powerful and dreaded Iranian rivals of Rome, and Herod and Phasael were unable to keep them out of Jerusalem. The shrewd Parthians installed Antigonus Mattathias, the last Hasmonaean High Priest, as Jewish ruler (40–37 BCE), and thus dealt a serious blow to Roman political ambitions in the Near East.[141] Phasael and the elderly Hyrcanus were handed over to Antigonus, and Phasael committed suicide.[142] Hyrcanus was taken to Parthia where he was well treated.[143]

Not strong enough to face up to Antigonus, let alone the Parthians, Herod escaped to Petra,[144] the Nabataean capital, whose dreamy image is perpetuated in the famous line of the nineteenth century poem by John William Burgon, 'a rose-red city half as old as time', and familiar also to cinema fans as the location where the denouement of the film, *Indiana Jones and the Last Crusade*, takes place.

6

Herod, king of the Jews (40–4 BCE)

From Petra, Herod continued his odyssey to Italy and Rome, via Egypt where he was entertained by Queen Cleopatra in Alexandria. In Rome, Mark Antony, convinced of Herod's military ability, persuaded his colleague Octavian, Julius Caesar's heir, and the Senate to appoint him king of Parthian-occupied Judaea. Accompanied by the two Roman leaders Octavian and Antony, Herod walked out of the Senate to attend a banquet given in his honour by Antony on the first day of his virtual reign.[145]

It took, however, three further years to convert this theoretical kingship into actual rule. Herod, the Idumaean upstart, had to depose an authentic scion of the Hasmonaean house, the High Priest-King Antigonus, who was moreover the protégé of the Parthian occupying power. This he achieved in 37 BCE with the military aid of two Roman legions, supplied and commanded by Sosius, governor of Syria.[146] In the course of the struggle with Antigonus's forces, Herod lost his brother Joseph, but true to himself he hastened to avenge his death on the enemy general Pappus, and sent the trophy of his severed head to his last surviving brother, Pheroras. Antigonus's only choice was to surrender to Sosius. He was taken in chains to Antioch in Syria where Antony, whose palm had been lavishly greased by Herod, ordered the last representative of the Hasmonaean power to be beheaded.[147]

The new king entered Jerusalem and, as his first royal act, he did his best to stop the Roman legionaries from pillaging the city and the Temple. Shrewdly and generously he rewarded the inhabitants of Jerusalem who, following the advice of the Pharisee Samaias (or Pollio), welcomed him to the city at the start of his reign and recognized him king of the Jews.[148]

Herod consolidates his rule (37–25 BCE)

The thirty-three year long reign of Herod falls into three parts. He spent the first twelve years on the consolidation of his rule. Although in possession of Jerusalem, Herod was fully aware of the hostility of the Jewish aristocracy and ruling classes, and felt the need to secure his future. Marriage into the Hasmonaean royal family appeared to be the most efficient and clever move. So, having dismissed his Nabataean wife, Doris, together with her son, Antipater, he took for spouse Mariamme, the beautiful granddaughter of the former High Priest and King/ethnarch, Hyrcanus II. She bore him three sons, Alexander and Aristobulus as well as a third son, who died young in Rome, and two daughters. Herod encouraged and facilitated the return of Hyrcanus, the grandfather of his new wife, from his Parthian captivity in Babylonia. His secret purpose was to keep an eye on and hold under his control this potential rival who was more entitled to the throne than Herod himself. Meanwhile the confiscation of the wealth of the hostile Jewish upper classes made him exceedingly rich and provided Herod with funds to pay for the continued goodwill of his Roman overlord, Mark Antony.

Herod's main immediate worry stemmed from the ambition of the queen of Egypt, Cleopatra VII, who was determined to expand her domains eastwards in the direction of Judaea and Nabataean Arabia. She used Antony's infatuation with her and managed to secure ownership on Herodian territory of the rich palm and balsam groves in the region of Jericho. Subsequently Herod had to pay her a substantial rent. The dates produced by the date palms of Jericho were much sought-after delicacies and the resin obtained from the balsam trees was a highly praised medicinal material in antiquity.[149]

Figure 6.1 *Coin of Cleopatra and Mark Antony.*

Cleopatra's ultimate aim was to bring about the downfall of both Herod and Malichus, king of Arabia, which she reckoned, would result in her inheriting both territories. On visiting Judaea in 34 BCE, the sensuous Cleopatra was toying with the idea of seducing Herod. 'It was never her nature to disguise the enjoyment of such pleasures', Josephus remarks.[150] However, in addition to fun, she may also have thought of using the bed as a trap. If found out, Herod would have been exposed to besotted Antony's furious retaliation, which would have served Cleopatra's plans. Herod, although not averse to the idea of getting rid of Cleopatra while she was in his power, followed his friends' advice and his own better judgement, and abstained from risking his patron's wrath.[151]

At the end, unwittingly, Cleopatra saved Herod's skin. In her greed for the possession of the Arab land, she persuaded Antony in 31 BCE to dispatch Herod with his army against the Nabataeans. In consequence of his engagement in this war, Herod could not be on Antony's side when he clashed with Octavian at the battle of Actium. As a result, Herod was not irreparably compromised in the eyes of the victorious Caesar Octavian.

If for a time Cleopatra was a serious headache for Herod, his marital bond with the Hasmonaeans was the cause of constant misery throughout the rest of his days. Hatred, intrigues, jealousy and plotting characterized the life of the members, above all of the female members, of Herod's court. The chief culprits on the one side of the household were Cypros and Salome, Herod's mother and his sister, and on the other, his wife

Mariamme with her mother Alexandra. The conflict allowed the Hasmonaean royals openly to display their disdain for the parvenu Idumaeans. Unavoidably catastrophe was approaching.

The first upheaval resulted from Herod's appointment of the undistinguished Babylonian priest Ananel to the vacant High Priestly office in replacement of the physically unfit Hyrcanus.[152] Alexandra, Herod's mother-in-law, was, however, determined to make sure that the pontificate went to her son Aristobulus, who, as the grandson of Hyrcanus, was in fact the legitimate claimant of the post. So she did what seemed natural in court circles. She made use of her friendship with Queen Cleopatra, and asked her to drop a word in her favour into the ear of Herod's political master, Antony.[153]

Cleopatra was persuasive and, as a result, Herod willy-nilly had to comply with Alexandra's design and, dismissing Ananel, he allowed the 17-year-old lad to assume the High Priestly office. However the loud and warm acclaim granted by the Jewish crowds in the Temple to Aristobulus, who was young and handsome as well as a true Hasmonaean, awakened Herod's envy and suspicion. Immediately he saw him as a threat, and in 35 BCE he engineered for him a swimming pool 'accident'. What was made to appear as horseplay between the High Priest and his young friends resulted in the drowning of Aristobulus in Jericho.[154]

Herod pretended to mourn his young brother-in-law, but he could not fool Alexandra. She sought revenge and obtained once again, with the help of Cleopatra, Antony's intervention. Herod was summoned to Alexandria and was asked to account for the young man's death. He smelled danger, foreseeing that his visit to Antony might turn out to be a one-way journey, and took appropriate measures, which in turn triggered off a whole series of tragedies. His uncle Joseph, who was also his brother-in-law, having married Salome, Herod's sister, was entrusted with the government of Judaea in his absence, but he was also secretly instructed to kill Mariamme, should Herod be put to death by Antony. His professed reason for this horrendous order was that he was so enamoured with her that even in death he wanted her to be in his company. In fact, he could not contemplate the prospect that his passionately loved wife should belong to someone else – and especially not to Mark Antony. He was indeed aware that Antony's sexual interest in Mariamme was deliberately awakened by Alexandra, who dispatched to him an alluring portrait of her daughter.[155]

Alexandra and Mariamme suspected that something was afoot and their adroitly handled feminine banter induced Joseph to let out the secret. The shocking discovery poisoned the Hasmonaean ladies' attitude towards Herod whom they had already held responsible for the death of young Aristobulus, and later for the assassination of the harmless old Hyrcanus, an unlikely rival, who was nevertheless strangled by Herod's order before his departure to see Octavian in 30 BCE. So when after talking, or rather bribing, himself out of trouble in Alexandria, he returned to Jerusalem and protested his love for Mariamme, she haughtily retorted: 'It was not the act of a lover to command that if he came to any harm, I too should be put to death.'[156]

To make things worse, Herod's sister, out of spite towards supercilious Mariamme and perhaps also wishing to dispose of her own husband, Joseph, insinuated to Herod that during his absence Mariamme and Joseph started an affair, and Mariamme learnt the secret order of putting her to death when they were in bed. She denied the charge and Herod relented his hostility towards her, but decided to execute his uncle/brother-in-law.[157]

The same scenario was repeated in connection with Mariamme and Soemus, the friend put in charge of the government of Judaea four years later in 30 BCE, when, after the battle of Actium, Herod took the lethal risk of visiting Octavian in Rhodes following the suicide of Antony. Mariamme and Alexandra lavished presents on Soemus and enticed him, as they did with Joseph on the previous occasion, to reveal to them the king's instructions. The usual channels of gossip by the Idumaean courtiers were used to poison Herod's attitude towards Mariamme. His feelings seesawed for a while, but at the end in 29 BCE he put to death Soemus and ordered a trial for his wife.[158]

Alexandra, sensing that she was equally in trouble, wished to dissociate herself publicly from her daughter. She grasped her by her hair and screamingly accused her of impudence in front of the whole court. Mariamme answered this sham display of disapproval with dignified silence.[159]

At the trial of Mariamme, Herod repeated the slanderous charges that she planned to poison him with love potions and drugs. Seeing the king going blind with fury, the members of the court quickly condemned Mariamme to death. Herod and some of the judges were thinking of imprisoning her first, but the vicious Salome and members of her entourage urged Herod to execute her without delay and avoid the chance of an uprising as the people held the queen to be innocent.

Josephus movingly portrays the end of Mariamme:

She bore herself calmly and kept her complexion . . . leaving the onlookers in no doubt of her noble breeding even in her last moments. Such was the death of Mariamme, a woman distinguished for her continence and magnanimity of character, though inclined to be . . . excessively quarrelsome. Words cannot do justice to her physical beauty and social presence . . . yet this was the principal reason for her failure to please the king . . . Courted by him constantly because of his love . . . she had an unbridled tongue. She was distressed by his treatment of her relatives, and saw fit to tell him all her feelings on the matter; and in the end she succeeded in making enemies not only of the king's mother and his sister, but of Herod himself, the one person she completely trusted to do her no harm.[160]

The killing of the woman whom he had madly loved completely unhinged Herod. His intellectual sanity appears to have gone. No diversion, such as parties, banquets, not even his favourite hunting expeditions, could keep Mariamme out of his mind. His mental imbalance – he kept on instructing servants to call her as though she were still alive – was followed by a severe illness, which Herod's physicians after many attempts were unable to treat and at the end left him to his own devices, but his strong constitution triumphed and he regained his strength.[161]

The next act of the drama occurred when Herod's recovery was still in the balance. Plotting the removal of Herod and a takeover of royal power, his mother-in-law Alexandra sought to persuade the officers in command of Jerusalem to hand over the government to her and her grandsons, the two sons of Herod borne by Mariamme. But the captains dutifully reported the matter to the king and this sounded the death knell for Alexandra in 28 BCE.[162] Thus ended the first act of the tragedy of the Hasmonaeans linked to Herod by matrimony: Aristobulus, Hyrcanus, Mariamme and Alexandra were put to death one after another.

Returning from the home front to politics, and stepping back a couple of years, the fall from grace of Mark Antony, first defeated by Caesar Octavian at Actium in 31 BCE and a second time in the following year in Egypt, rendered the chances of survival of the kingship of Herod extremely precarious. Being, however, one of the most astute politicians of his age, he was conscious of this state of affairs and devised an audacious plan, a kind of tightrope walking, which, if successful, might ensure his future. Herod handed over the reins of government to his younger brother Pheroras, and unannounced and uninvited he sailed to the island of Rhodes in the hope of having an audience with Octavian. Removing from his head the royal diadem, he endeavoured to surprise the ruler of Rome and gain his sympathy by appearing before him as a humble commoner and confessing to him the truth and the whole truth.

Figure 6.2 *Bronze bust of Octavian/ Augustus.*

Following the accounts preserved in both the *Jewish War* and the *Jewish Antiquities* of Josephus, Herod did not conceal, indeed firmly proclaimed, his past closeness to Antony, the man to whom he owed his crown. He acknowledged that he went on to the end providing him with auxiliary troops and a large quantity of foodstuff, not forgetting quietly to mention that he himself and his main army, detained by his conflict with the Nabataeans, did not constitute a threat to Octavian at Actium. Even after Antony's defeat, he remained on his side as a counsellor, but Antony was too infatuated with Cleopatra to listen to his sensible advice and get rid of the 'fatal monster' (the *fatale monstrum* to use Horace's poetic definition of Cleopatra),[163] who was the principal cause of his downfall. Josephus quotes or invents Herod's peroration full of great rhetorical potency:

I am come to rest my safety on my integrity . . . I am not ashamed to declare my loyalty to Antony. But if you would disregard the individual concerned, and examine how I requite my benefactors, and how staunch a friend I prove, then you may know me by the test of my past actions. I hope that the subject of inquiry will be not whose friend, but how loyal a friend, I have been.[164]

The audacious gambit worked; Octavian was impressed and he restored the diadem to Herod's head, apparently with the words:

So staunch a champion of the claims of friendship deserves to be ruler over many subjects ... Antony did well in obeying Cleopatra's behests rather than yours; for through his folly we have gained you.[165]

These words were confirmed by an official decree and, as a visible proof of his favour with Octavian, Herod was allowed to ride beside him across Syria on his way to Egypt. On entering his own kingdom at Ptolemais, Herod prepared a lavish reception for Caesar and again rode next to him when he reviewed his troops. A further gift of 800 talents, a sum thought to be in excess of Herod's real means, sealed their bond for good. Herod was thought to be Octavian's second best friend immediately after Marcus

Vipsanius Agrippa, and Agrippa's second best friend preceded only by Caesar. After the grave internal and external turmoil of the past years, the future of the Herodian kingship looked to stand on solid foundations. Not only were the territories annexed by Cleopatra returned to Judaea, but Herod also received several Palestinian cities, including Samaria and Strato's Tower, which was soon to be renamed Caesarea.[166] His kingdom included Idumaea (part of present day Negev), Judaea and Samaria as well as various Transjordanian territories in the north-east, Trachonitis, Batanaea and Auranitis (Southern Syria and Northern Jordan) that were donated to him by Augustus. The friendship between Caesar and Herod came only once under a cloud. In 7 BCE Herod led a military expedition against the Nabataeans, which the Emperor considered unauthorized, but the clever and tactful diplomacy of Nicolas of Damascus ironed out the misunderstanding and friendly relations were re-established at once.[167]

His friendship with Octavian, surnamed Augustus since 27 BCE, enabled Herod to send to Rome in 23/22 BCE his two sons by Mariamme, Alexander and Aristobulus, in order to ensure for them an education appropriate to their princely rank.[168] They were received by Herod's friend Pollio, probably the historian and former consul in 40 BCE, C. Asinius Pollio, and stayed in his house. Occasionally they even resided with Augustus himself in the imperial palace. The two young men returned to Jerusalem some five years later in the company of their father, at the end of Herod's second visit to the capital of the Empire in 18/17 BCE.

Herod, the builder (25–13 BCE)

The second epoch of Herod's reign is chiefly distinguished by the splendour of his architectural projects. Without a doubt, he was the greatest builder in the Holy Land, planning and overseeing the execution of palaces, fortresses, theatres, amphitheatres, harbours and the entire city of Caesarea, and to crown them all, he organized the rebuilding of the Temple of Jerusalem. His enterprises displayed Hellenistic and Roman influence consonant with his aim to integrate his kingdom into the Empire of Augustus

without upsetting Jewish sensibilities. His personal contribution consisted in the choice
of the sites and the planning of the projects. What has survived of his architectural
masterpieces constitutes in a sense the most direct testimony of the true Herod.

This period started with a bad omen. A famine, resulting from an extended drought
in 25–24 BCE, delayed by a couple of years the start of his grandiose enterprises.
Witnessing the sufferings of the population, Herod set out immediately to purchase
with moneys obtained from the sale of his own valuables large quantities of food from
Egypt and distributed it to the starving inhabitants not only of Judaea, but even to
people living in some of the cities of Syria beyond the frontiers of his kingdom. His
generosity ensured for him for a time the sympathy of the otherwise generally unfriendly
Jewish population. In their eyes Herod still appeared as the usurper of the throne of the
Hasmonaeans, to whom the people remained attached. Similar politically inspired
benevolence culminated in the remission of one-third of the taxes to help economic
recovery after the famine and some ten years later in 14 BCE the same gesture was
repeated, this time rescinding one-quarter of the tributes due to the king, thus
demonstrating the success of his rule and his care for his subjects. Yet, despite
performing all these acts of benevolence, Herod never felt totally at home with Jews
and was much more at ease in the company of Greeks.[169]

The purpose of the architectural projects of Herod was partly to provide security for
himself and his family in the eventuality of a rebellion through the construction of
palaces and palace fortresses, and partly to increase his fame inside his kingdom and
in the outside Roman world through building activity honouring the Emperor. Such
was the work accomplished at Samaria which he renamed Sebaste, the August City,
from the Greek for Augustus (Sebastos), and by the creation of Caesarea (Caesar's City)
and its port, providing his kingdom with a wide opening to Mediterranean commerce
and culture.

In Jerusalem, he reinforced the royal palace and erected, before the fall of Mark
Antony, the Fortress Antonia next to the Temple, from where at the same time he could
command the whole Temple Mount.

Samaria was turned into a stronghold. Herod also enriched it with a temple dedicated
to the Emperor and provided it with a forum.[170]

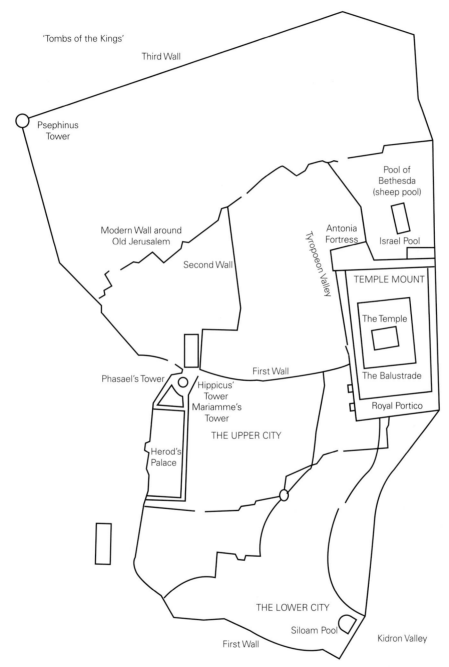

'Tombs of the Kings'

Third Wall

Psephinus
Tower

Pool of
Bethesda
(sheep pool)

Modern Wall around
Old Jerusalem

Antonia
Fortress

Israel Pool

Tyropoeon Valley

Second Wall

TEMPLE MOUNT

The Temple

Phasael's Tower

First Wall

The Balustrade

Hippicus'
Tower
Mariamme's
Tower

Royal Portico

THE UPPER CITY

Herod's
Palace

THE LOWER CITY

Siloam Pool

Kidron Valley

First Wall

Figure 6.3 *Map of the city of Jerusalem in the Herodian period.*

Figure 6.4 *Herod's palace in Jerusalem.*

Among the desert fortresses built or rebuilt by Herod, Masada was unquestionably the most outstanding. It was first fortified by Alexander Jannaeus (103–76 BCE), but Herod developed it into a spectacular rock stronghold on an impregnable-looking 400 m high cliff, about 5 km west of the Dead Sea. During his escape from Jerusalem from the Parthians in 40 BCE, Herod left there the female members of his family, according to Josephus.[171] Immediately on becoming king of Judaea from 37 to 31 BCE he started a major building programme including the installation of a reliable water system and the construction of two palaces. The Northern palace with splendid mosaics and a luxurious garden, with a bathhouse, a garrison edifice, storehouses and a purification pool, is considered to be the jewel of his architectural projects. The containers found there by archaeologists reveal the gourmet lifestyle adopted by the king and shared with his eminent guests. The best of the fine wines the Aegean islands of Chios and Cos and the vineyards of southern Italy could produce reached the desert fortress and, to please his Roman guests, Herod imported for them the much fancied apples of Italy.[172]

Figure 6.5 *A Herodian mansion in Jerusalem.*

The conquest of Masada demanded all the strategic skill of the Romans.[173] The fortress, one of the rooms of which was converted into a synagogue by the rebels,[174] fell in 73/74 CE after the Zealot commander ordered his men to kill their own families, then one another, altogether 960 persons.

In Jerusalem, in 19 BCE, Herod started probably the greatest, and as far as his relation to Judaism was concerned the most significant, of his building ventures

Figure 6.6 *The 2nd/3rd century forum in Sebaste/Samaria, most probably built over the top of Herod's forum.*

with the reconstruction at his own expense of the Temple. In its final form the Second Temple is known as Herod's Temple. The monumental section of it that still survives is the famous Western (or Wailing) Wall in Jerusalem, a glorious memorial of the past for some, and the most holy place of Jewish worship for others.

The size of the edifice of the Second Temple, built at the end of the sixth century BCE following the return from the Babylonian exile, was substantially enlarged and its height raised.[175] The inhabitants of Jerusalem, though impressed by Herod's plans, were nevertheless worried that he might pull down the existing building and then run out of means before completing the new one.

To reassure them, Herod assembled in advance all the necessary monumental stones and wood materials, hired and trained stonemasons and carpenters, among whom was

Figure 6.7, facing page *Masada.*

Figure 6.9 *The bathhouse in Masada. This image shows the Caldarium (hot room). The floor is suspended on pillars. Hot air was pumped under the floor, which heated the waters. This is known as the hypocaust method. The pipes running up the walls enabled the hot air to warm up the side of the pool. The lavish Roman style of Herod's bathhouse shows how impressive this palace would have been.*

a certain Simon whose ossuary was discovered in Jerusalem with an Aramaic inscription describing him as 'the Temple builder'.[176]

To allay the religious concerns of the traditionalists, he associated the Jewish priests and Levites with the design and the execution of the project. To cap it all, he ordered sumptuous robes for one thousand priests. The main sanctuary was speedily completed in eighteen months and was inaugurated with a grandiose ceremony at which Herod ordered the slaughter of 300 sacrificial oxen.

Figure 6.8, facing page *Mosaic in Masada.*

Figure 6.10 *The Western (or Wailing) Wall of the Temple.*

Figure 6.11 *Ossuary with Aramaic inscription: Simon the Temple builder.*

The Temple of Jerusalem was celebrated as one of the marvels of the ancient world. Herod proudly showed it to Marcus Agrippa, his and Augustus's close friend, when he visited Jerusalem in 15 BCE. On that occasion, Agrippa ordered the offering of a hecatomb, a sacrifice of 100 oxen, to the God of the Jews. To commemorate this great event, by order of the king, Agrippa's name was engraved on one of the gates of the Temple. The boundaries of the sanctuary that non-Jews were forbidden to cross were marked by warning inscriptions in Greek, some of which have survived, threatening any culprit with instant death:

No foreigner is to enter within the balustrade and forecourt around the sacred precinct. Whoever is caught will himself be responsible for (his) consequent death.[177]

According to Josephus, there were also warnings in Latin.[178]

Figure 6.12 *Model of Herod's Temple in Jerusalem. Scholars differ on how accurate this is as a representation of the Temple, but it does something to capture the size and impact this great building would have had.*

Construction work went on throughout the remainder of Herod's reign and for a long time after his death in 4 BCE. In fact, the building operations did not reach completion until the procuratorship of Albinus (62–4 CE),[179] shortly before the destruction of the sanctuary at the end of the siege of Jerusalem by Titus in 70 CE.

Among Herod's achievements in or close to Jerusalem, Josephus mentions in addition to the Temple, the royal palace and the Phasael tower, named after his brother, also a theatre, an amphitheatre and a hippodrome, the latter three no doubt catering for the progressive Hellenized taste of the not strictly religious Jews inhabiting or visiting the city.[180]

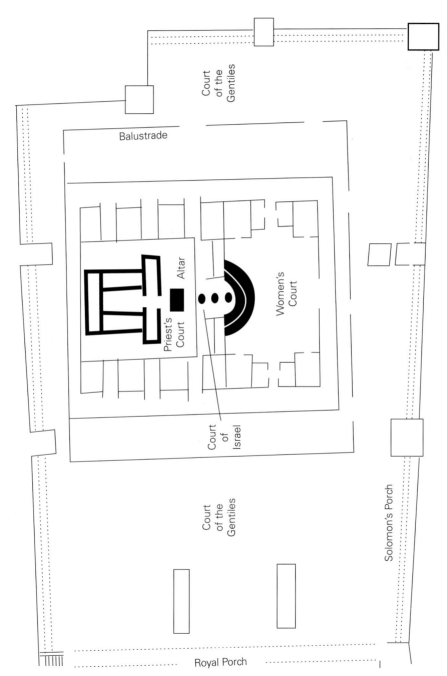

Figure 6.13 *Plan of Herod's Temple in Jerusalem.*

Figure 6.14 *Greek inscription on the partition wall of the Temple threatening non-Jewish entrants with instant death.*

In addition to glorifying the sacred Temple of Judaism, Herod was also determined to perpetuate the memory of the members of his family, not forgetting his own. He built the coastal town of Antipatris (Aphek) between Caesarea and Jerusalem to honour his father. A fortress named Cypros after his mother was erected near Jericho, and the city of Phasaelis, also in the Jericho area, as well as the already mentioned Phasael tower in Jerusalem, preserved his brother's name for posterity.

In Jericho, Herod erected a most refined palace with four wings, large halls and luxurious gardens. He built there also colonnades, the greatest pool discovered in Palestine (90 by 42 m), a dining room for large banquets (29 by 19 m), reception rooms and a throne room, all decorated with frescoes displaying floral patterns.[181]

Finally, to perpetuate his own name and his glory, he created Herodium about 10 miles south-east of Bethlehem on a 60 acres site. To quote Josephus, Herodium stands on a hill with 'its summit raised artificially and rounded like a woman's breast, with circular towers at intervals, which is approached by a steep staircase of 200 steps, made from specially fashioned stones.'[182] The choice of the place was motivated by a

Figure 6.15 *Map of Herod's kingdom.*

Figure 6.16 *The Phasael tower built by Herod in Jerusalem. Originally there were two more towers, one dedicated to Mariamme and another to Hippicus. After the destruction of Jerusalem in 70 AD only the Phasael tower remained. Its present shape owes much to later Muslim and Crusader rule.*

search for security, yet still close to the capital, and a palace standing on the top of a mountain seemed to be appropriate for a king. To secure water supply in this desert location, he had to build a 6 km long aqueduct.

Herodium was a magnificent sight with its four towers and beautiful halls decorated with non-figurative wall paintings. On the slope of the mountain a small, intimate theatre was constructed for an audience of 300 to 400 spectators, and as a Herodian innovation to Graeco-Roman theatre architecture, a dining room was attached to it to entertain the royal family and significant guests.

But in the king's mind Herodium was to be also his final resting place. A mausoleum was erected there, three storeys high (c. 25 m) made of white limestone. Israeli archaeologists, led by Ehud Netzer, thoroughly investigated the site and, in 2007, Netzer claimed that he had identified among the ruins parts of a large empty sarcophagus, made of Jerusalemite reddish limestone with exceptional craftsmanship, and decorated with rosettes. Broken into hundreds of pieces in antiquity, possibly by Jewish revolutionaries who detested his memory, it once contained, in Netzer's view, the remains of Herod.[183] Netzer himself, after many years of digging at Herodium, met his death there accidentally falling from a platform in October 2010.

Outside the strictly Jewish areas of his kingdom, Herod played the enlightened Hellenist monarch and built or enriched pagan cities and promoted Graeco-Roman art, architecture and culture. After the Jerusalem Temple, the city of Caesarea represents the climax of his personal creative activity. It was constructed between 23/22 and 10 BCE with no expense spared in place of the old and decrepit town known as Strato's Tower on the non-Jewish Mediterranean coast of his realm. Imported white marble was used everywhere in the construction of the palaces and the pagan temples. An imposing harbour, which according to Josephus matched the size of Piraeus, the port of Athens,[184] was the most admired feature of the new city. It was 'the largest artificial harbour ever built in the open sea up to that point'.[185]

To provide water for the inhabitants, Herod constructed a magnificent giant aqueduct, which still stands today. Caesarea comprised a theatre, a hippodrome and a racetrack built for quinquennial games to be held in honour of the Emperor, as well as a statue of Caesar and a temple dedicated to him. A Latin inscription mentioning Pontius Pilate was discovered in the theatre.[186] A private royal palace, referred to also as the praetorium, was erected on a promontory into the Mediterranean not far from the theatre, equipped, as would be expected, with a swimming pool.

According to the New Testament, St Paul spent some time as a prisoner in that same praetorium,[187] and was summoned from his cell by the Roman procurator Porcius Festus to entertain in 60 CE Herod's great-grandson King Agrippa II and his sister Berenice,[188] the Herodian princess who was to become the lover of Titus,[189] the conqueror of Jerusalem and Roman Emperor, after his father Vespasian, from 79 to 81 CE.

Herod's architectural and cultural activity extended far beyond the frontiers of his kingdom. At Paneas, near the sources of the Jordan River, later renamed Caesarea

Figure 6.17 *Herodium, 'rounded like a woman's breast' (Josephus).*

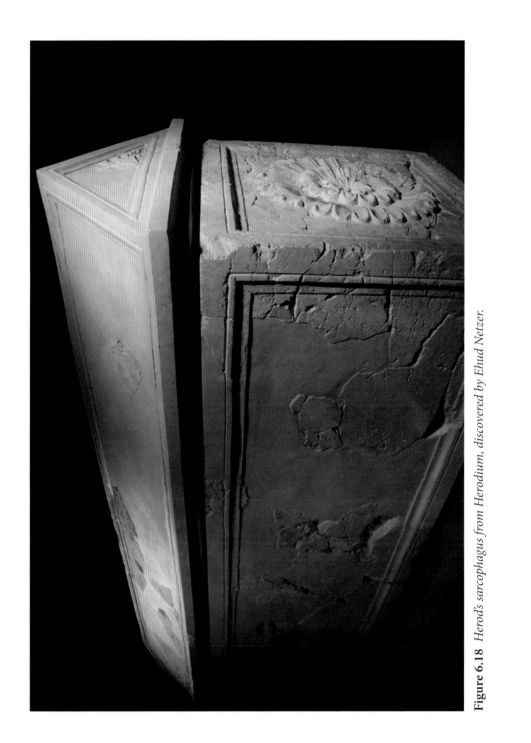

Figure 6.18 *Herod's sarcophagus from Herodium, discovered by Ehud Netzer.*

Figure 6.19 *The Harbour of Caesarea.*

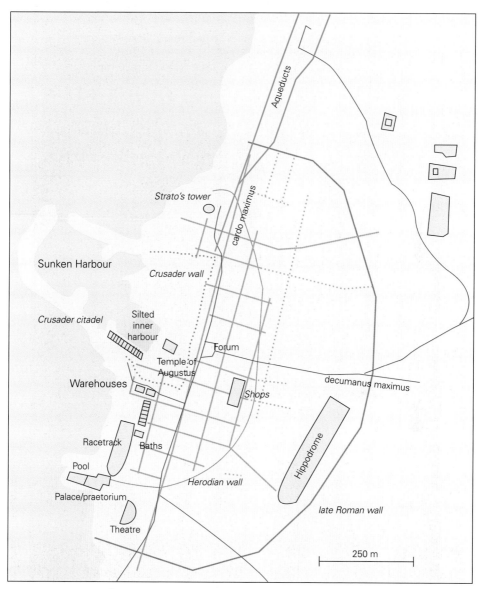

Figure 6.20 *Map of Caesarea.*

Figure 6.21 *The Aqueduct at Caesarea. It was originally over 10 km long and brought water from the south side of Mount Carmel to Caesarea for around 1200 years.*

Figure 6.22 *The racetrack at Caesarea, originally built by Herod to celebrate the opening of the city.*

Figure 6.23 *The Pilate inscription from the theatre at Caesarea. This is the only unanimously acknowledged archaeological find containing an inscription mentioning 'Pontius Pilatus' that has been discovered to date.*

Philippi, where St Peter would supposedly confess the messianic dignity of Jesus, Herod erected another temple, made of white marble, to honour Augustus.[190]

Herod also built or reconstructed temples in Lebanon at Berytus (Beirut) and Tyre, as well as on the Aegean island of Rhodes where he also supported shipbuilding. He financed the creation of gymnasia for athletes in Tripolis, Damascus and Ptolemais, and erected theatres in Sidon and Damascus, baths and fountains in the Palestinian Hellenistic city of Ascalon, and an aqueduct in Laodicea in Syria. He also beautified the main street of Antioch in Syria, paving it with polished marble and providing it with a colonnade. Countless other towns in the Greek world benefitted from the Jewish king's love of beautiful buildings. His munificence, too, extended far and wide. To mention but a few cases, he endowed in perpetuity the post of the administrator of the gymnasium on the island of Cos, and gave to the city of Elis/

Figure 6.24 *An architectural fragment identified by some as coming from the temple of Augustus at Paneas (Caesarea Philippi).*

Olympia in Greece a large sum of money for the financial support of the quadrennial Olympic games, the survival of which was threatened by lack of funds.

As the London Olympics are still in one's memory, it may be apposite to mention that, in gratitude for his generosity, the organizers of the ancient games elected Herod perpetual Olympic president and recorded it in inscriptions. Herod actually fulfilled his presidential privilege in person when he attended the competitions of the 192nd Olympic games in the course of his journey to Rome in 12 BCE.[191] If Baron Pierre de Coubertin founded in 1896 the modern Olympiads, Herod must be celebrated as the saviour of the ancient competitions. Thanks to his liberality, the quadrennial confrontation of athletes survived for nearly another 400 years after his death and came to an end only in 385 CE in the days of the Christian Emperor Theodosius the Great.

Herod's decline (13–4 BCE)

The middle period (25–13 BCE) constituted the glory days of Herod's reign. By the end of this epoch, he was in his sixties. Buttressed by the friendship of Augustus and Agrippa,

Figure 6.25 *Spring at Caesarea Philippi.*

Herod seemed to be set for a safe and happy old age, though according to the cheeky remark of his son Alexander, he did not want to look old and tried to disguise his advanced age by dying his hair black. Not counting the star-crossed Mariamme, Herod had no fewer than nine living wives. Josephus explains to his Gentile readers that polygamy was not forbidden by Jewish law and tradition. In fact, in the case of kings, it could be practiced on a lavish scale and according to the Mishnah, it was extended to as many as eighteen wives, though the rigorist members of the Essene sect described in the Dead Sea Scrolls stipulated monogamy all round, even in the case of the Jewish king.[192] In 14 BCE, even Doris, Herod's repudiated first spouse, regained favour and was readmitted to the court together with Herod's eldest son. Previously the firstborn Antipater was permitted to visit Jerusalem only on the occasion of the three great Jewish festivals: Passover, the Feast of Weeks and the feast of Tabernacles.

The remaining eight wives bore Herod five further sons. The Samaritan Malthace was the mother of Archelaus, who succeeded Herod as ruler (ethnarch) of Judaea,[193] and of Antipas who governed Galilee as tetrarch in the lifetime of Jesus.[194] Another wife, the second Mariamme, daughter of the High Priest Boethus, gave birth to a son referred to simply as Herod. Two further sons, another Herod and Philip, were the children of Cleopatra of Jerusalem, and they were brought up in Rome. In addition, the royal household included Pheroras, Herod's younger brother, and his wife, whom Herod intensely disliked. Last but not least, there was Salome, the sister devoted to Herod, but a constant schemer towards the others, and her latest (third) husband, Alexas. She had got rid of two earlier ones, Joseph and Costobar, with the helping hand of her brother.

There were also the three rival male siblings. On the one hand, we find the elder brother, Antipater, married to the daughter of Antigonus, the last inglorious Hasmonaean High Priest-King, and on the other hand, Alexander and Aristobulus, the two sons of the Jewish princess Mariamme. The former was married to Glaphyra, the daughter of the Cappadocian king Archelaus, and the latter to his cousin, Berenice, the daughter of Herod's sister Salome.[195]

Far from being a peaceful and loving patriarchal family, Herod's household rather resembled a hornets' nest. A female clique was formed by Herod's sister-in-law, the wife of Pheroras, together with her mother and sister, and the king's first wife, Doris. They did their best in clandestine gatherings to manipulate and harass the rest of the family. At daggers drawn with them, Salome, Herod's malicious sister, quietly spied on them and reported their machinations to the king. Herod, putting the principal blame on Pheroras's wife, ordered his brother either to divorce his wife or leave the royal palace. The strong-minded Pheroras refused to dismiss his spouse and preferred to withdraw to his own territory in Peraea.[196]

The infighting of the ladies of the court was a mere storm in a teacup compared with the troubles fomented by Antipater's duplicitous schemes aimed at eliminating from the line of royal succession Alexander and Aristobulus, the favourite sons of Herod. The two princes in their twenties, with Jewish royal blood and pride in their veins and having inherited their mother's unbridled tongue, considered themselves superior to Antipater, whose mother, Doris, lacked class compared with the Hasmonaean Mariamme. The two young men naturally felt bitter towards Herod for killing their mother (and their uncle, Aristobulus, as well as their grandmother, Alexandra, and their great-grandfather, Hyrcanus) and openly aired their grievances against their father. The malevolent and manipulative Antipater kept on informing the king. He slanderously reported that his two brothers were plotting regicide, an accusation that was echoed by the equally vicious gossip of Salome and Pheroras, Herod's sister and brother. So in order to put Alexander and Aristobulus in their places, Herod went on raising the status of his 'devoted' firstborn, Antipater. He named him his heir in his first will, and sent him to Rome with warm recommendations to Augustus. As the atmosphere grew more and more poisonous and sinister, in 12 BCE Herod took Alexander and Aristobulus to Rome and accused them before Caesar of treacherously plotting against his life. Alexander, a brilliant orator, delivered a powerful apology in which he clearly stated that Antipater was the cause of the discord in the family and convinced Augustus of his and his brother's innocence. The peace-loving Emperor used his influence on Herod and effected a family reconciliation. As a result, father and sons returned to Jerusalem, but Antipater did not fall out of favour. Herod, thanking God and Caesar for the new peace in the household, proclaimed all his three sons jointly kings, but with priority given to Antipater, an arrangement that did not please or satisfy any of them.

While Antipater pretended to be delighted, Alexander and Aristobulus visibly resented the primogenital right granted to their senior half-brother. In turn, Antipater was secretly fuming because his rivals were not stripped of their royal rank. The scandal-mongering by Antipater, accompanied by the slanderous insinuations of Pheroras and Salome, came to a fresh boiling point. Herod subjected Alexander's friends to torture and one of them broke down and accused the young man of conspiracy against Herod. In his prison cell, Alexander wrote a long document of self-defence in which he named Pheroras and Salome as the real guilty parties. The aunt was even accused of entering Alexander's bedroom and forcing him to have sex with her. The new crisis was resolved by the diplomatic play-acting of King Archelaus of Cappadocia, Alexander's father-in-law. He feigned to be upset and furious with his son-in-law for his abominable behaviour and threatened to terminate his marriage by taking home his daughter Glaphyra. Meanwhile he cleverly shifted the blame onto Pheroras. Herod swallowed the bait and instinctively took the side of his son. Thus calm was established again for a short while.[197]

The final act of the tragedy was sparked off by a travelling Spartan adventurer by the name of Eurycles, who, in order to repay an obligation he owed to Antipater, extolled his praises before Herod and at the same time denounced Alexander and Aristobulus as treacherous plotters.[198] Also to rekindle the king's hostility against the sons of Mariamme, Salome reported to her brother that according to the gossip spread by Aristobulus, Herod was planning to kill her. The king went totally berserk, jailed both princes in separate cells, and formally charged them with treason before Augustus. By that time, as has been noted, the temporary breach between him and the Emperor, caused by Herod's invasion of Arabia, was mended by the clever diplomacy of Nicolas of Damascus, and the friendship with Augustus was restored. So the Emperor considered the king's complaint and, while sorry for Alexander and Aristobulus, whom he knew well from their student days in Rome partly spent in the imperial household, he did not feel justified to deprive a king of the right to deal with his own sons. Augustus agreed that they were to be appropriately punished if the charge of planned parricide was proven, but simply admonished if they only wanted to escape from paternal control. To judge Alexander and Aristobulus, Herod was instructed to convoke a council in Berytus (Beirut), which should comprise Roman dignitaries and the king's friends. Herod's chief adviser, Nicolas of Damascus, also hoped that Herod would jail rather than execute his sons, adding that most of his friends in Rome voiced a similar, lenient opinion.

The court was then summoned. Saturninus, governor of Syria, was the presiding judge, assisted by other Roman officials. Herod himself, his brother Pheroras and sister Salome, and other Syrian leading personalities sat with them, but King Archelaus, Alexander's father-in-law, whom Herod distrusted, was not invited. The accused sons were not summoned either to present their defence. Saturninus and his three sons found Alexander and Aristobulus guilty, but not of a capital crime.[199] Herod, however, and all the other members of the council including one of the Roman dignitaries, voted for the death penalty. In Sebaste, where Herod married Mariamme thirty years earlier, their two sons were executed by strangulation in 7 BCE. Their bodies were taken to Alexandrion, some 30 miles south-east of Samaria, to be buried next to their maternal grandfather Alexander, son of the High Priest Aristobulus II.

In spite of the hatred of the Jews, who knew that he was truly responsible for the murder of the princes, Antipater imagined that he was in the clear and could have the last laugh. He chose for his next target his five nephews, children of the executed Alexander and Aristobulus, whom the remorseful Herod, trying to appear as a loving grandfather, treated with warmth and sympathy. Through his usual flattery, Antipater persuaded Herod to rearrange his grandsons' planned marriages so that his own interests should be protected. Thus reassured, he felt free to set sail to Rome in 6 BCE in order to establish useful connections in the imperial court. He carried with him his father's will in which he was designated as heir to the throne.[200]

Yet the fateful day of reckoning in its unpredictable way was fast approaching. The exiled Pheroras, Herod's youngest brother, died, and it was reported to Herod that he was poisoned by a love potion administered to him by Doris, Antipater's mother. So Doris again fell out of favour and was repudiated for a second time, and tortured servants of the palace confessed that the poison was not prepared for Pheroras, nor was it administered to him. On the contrary, it was Pheroras together with Antipater who acquired it and was actually meant for none other than Herod. Slaves and courtiers were interrogated under torture and they let it be known where the hidden, still unused, poison could be retrieved. All the evidence was now pointing at Antipater. By then he was in Rome and knew nothing of the discovery of his duplicitous stratagems in Jerusalem. Consequently, he took at face value the seemingly affectionate tone of Herod's letter, in which he urged his son to return without delay as he intended to pardon his mother on his arrival. Antipater was taken in and promptly embarked for Caesarea.[201]

On arrival, he was cold-shouldered by all and sundry, as his fall from grace had by then become common knowledge. Antipater realized that he was in deep trouble, but he still hoped that he would be able to extricate himself through lies, sycophancy and deceit, but this time it was too late. Herod rejected his approach, threw him into prison and ordered him to prepare his defence as he was to appear next day before a tribunal, chaired by Publius Quinctilius Varus, the Roman governor of Syria, who was visiting Jerusalem and whom Herod had made privy to the situation. In the presence of Herod's relations and associates and Antipater's own friends, informers laid out their charges. Giving no chance to his son to defend himself, the king indicted him for attempted parricide and for engineering the downfall of his brothers. Herod then invited Nicolas of Damascus to read out in full the prosecution's case against Antipater, whom he compared to a particularly venomous snake. The accused denied the charges and argued that he had no reason to seek the removal of his father as he was already exercising royal power all but in name. Furthermore, he claimed, he was universally admired for his filial piety, and even Augustus referred to him as 'Father lover' (*Philopator*). With crocodile tears in his eyes, he volunteered for torture to prove his innocence.[202]

He nearly succeeded. The members of the court, including Varus, were taken in, but Herod remained adamant of his son's guilt. Asked for a last word in his defence, Antipater could only call on God to be his witness. Then came the final act of the court drama: the poison, obtained by Antipater and intended for Herod, was administered to a criminal already under capital sentence. He drank it and immediately dropped dead. Varus did no longer hesitate. He formulated his death sentence in writing and the document was sent to Augustus, while Antipater was kept in irons.[203]

Finally Augustus's letter arrived, confirming Antipater's death sentence unless Herod would be contented simply to banish him. Herod remained inexorable. Antipater even at this stage, in the mistaken belief that his father had already died, sought to bribe his way out of prison, but the chief gaoler informed Herod who, with a scream believed to be beyond a dying man's strength, sent some of his bodyguard with the order to execute Antipater at once and bury him without honour in nearby Hyrcania.

Herod's condition was worsening. He wrote a new will and, disinheriting Antipater, he named Antipas his heir in preference to his elder son Archelaus. He also made large bequests to the Emperor, the Empress and their children as well as to members of his own family, above all his sister, Salome, to whom he left also the cities of Jamnia and Azotus on the Mediterranean coast and Phasaelis with its precious palm groves north of Jericho.

But Herod was not allowed to depart peacefully. While it was whispered that the king was dying, two renowned and much loved teachers of the Mosaic Law, Judas, the son of Seriphaeus, and Matthias, the son of Margalothus, exhorted their pupils to climb to the roof of the Temple and pull down and destroy the golden eagle, symbol of Rome, affixed to the sanctuary by order of Herod. Incensed with rage at hearing the news, the king almost forgot his sickness and was carried to a public gathering. He condemned the two instigators to be burned alive and sentenced to death the forty young men who participated in the affair.[204] An eclipse of the moon on the following night indicated heavenly displeasure in the eyes of the ordinary inhabitants of Jerusalem.[205]

By then the king's illness reached its final stage and Herod's body began to disintegrate. He suffered from fever, skin disease, gangrene, inflammation, convulsions and asthma. This is how Josephus describes Herod's final condition, a portrait that seems to be influenced to some extent by the literary cliché regarding the dreadful death of tyrants:

He had a mild fever, showing little evidence of inflammation to the touch but accompanied by serious internal disorder, one of the symptoms being a desperate and compulsive urge to get relief by scratching himself. He suffered ulceration of his bowels, with acute intestinal pains, and an effusion of colourless fluid around the feet. He had a similar disorder of the abdomen, and what is more, a gangrene of the genitals that produced worms. He had difficulty in getting his breath when sitting upright, and his breathing was extremely unpleasant because of the offensive nature of the exhalation and his constant gasping. And in every limb he experienced convulsions that became unbearably violent.[206]

Popular wisdom saw in his worsening condition divine punishment for his wickedness, manifested in particular in the recent execution of the two saintly teachers of the Law. His doctors advised as a last resort a journey to the eastern side of the Dead Sea to seek relief at the celebrated thermal hot springs of Callirrhoe. However, as the treatment with oil nearly killed him, they all returned to Jericho. There Herod was stopped from committing suicide. He attempted to kill himself with a knife, which he was given to peel fruit and cut it to small pieces.[207]

Herod had only five more days left to live, and died shortly before Passover in 4 BCE,[208] but he still did not stop. He rewrote his will for a third and last time, and appointed his eldest surviving son Archelaus as king, but this proposal was not confirmed by the Emperor, who did not grant royal dignity to Archelaus and reduced his status to that of an ethnarch or national ruler. Then, or perhaps somewhat earlier, Herod devised a devilish exit ritual for himself. He ordered the arrest of all the leading men of Judaea and their incarceration in the hippodrome of Jericho. Convinced that his passing would be a cause of rejoicing for many Jews, he instructed his sister Salome and her husband Alexas to issue an order for the massacre of all the prisoners in the hippodrome, immediately after his death, but before the news reached the public. 'Let all Judaea and every household weep for me, whether they will or no', was his last directive.[209] Salome, guilty of countless wicked deeds in her life, mustered the courage to disobey him this time: in direct breach of her brother's last wish, she threw the gates of the hippodrome open and released all the imprisoned Jewish leaders. She even lied to them declaring that this was the wish of Herod, who had changed his mind.

The body of Herod was transported in all magnificence to its final resting place in a bier of solid gold covered with royal purple. On it lay the deceased, also clothed in purple, with his crown, diadem and sceptre. The sons and relatives walked beside the body, followed by his fully armed bodyguards, his mercenaries from Thrace, Germany and Gaul, and the rest of the army arranged in battle formations. The military cortege and 500 spice-carrying royal slaves and freedmen proceeded from Jericho and accompanied the bier for the first eight stades (1 mile). The journey then continued on the 25-mile-long road to Herodium, the carefully planned place of rest for Herod the Great, king of the Jews.[210]

7

Herod the Villain or Herod the Great?

After this outline of the story of Herod, all that now remains is to sketch his portrait, assess his personality, evaluate his character and, above all, determine his significance in the minds of his contemporaries as well as in the history of Judaism and Christianity.

The portrait of Herod

As far as his physical appearance is concerned, unfortunately no image of Herod has survived, so the only way one can hypothetically reconstruct his portrait is through recovering the family resemblance by looking at the coins of his grandsons, Herod of Chalcis and Herod Agrippa I, and the latter's son, King Agrippa II (see Chapters 11 to 13). All the other details are borrowed from Josephus's descriptions.

In appearance Herod was a powerful and athletic man though he does not seem to have been particularly tall. He clearly did not match the height of his son Alexander, who felt obliged to stoop when they walked together so as to appear smaller than his father. It seems that he could not tolerate that anyone should exceed him in any way. He was an excellent rider and in hunting no one was, or was permitted to appear, his equal. One day he is said to have killed as many as forty stags, boars and wild asses. Here again the same son Alexander felt the need deliberately to miss the prey on occasion so as not to give the impression that he was a better shot than the king.[211] Herod was also an outstanding soldier. Few could match his precision as a javelin thrower or an archer. From his early triumphant campaign in Galilee against Ezechias and his brigands to his handling of the Nabataean conflict when he was a sexagenarian, he proved to be a brilliant general. His armies were almost always victorious when he was personally in charge of the action.

Herod's character

Herod was a many-faceted personality. His qualities were gigantic; so were also his defects. He knew he was extremely lucky to become king, but his success owed much to his good judgement too. As a politician he was endowed with exceptional gifts. His most admirable achievement was the perfect handling of the extremely dangerous meeting with Octavian in Rhodes in 30 BCE (see Chapter 6). He was always a faithful servant of Rome, but he knew also how to reward those who had pleased him or rendered service to him. He was generous to the Pharisees and the Essenes, but anyone who antagonized him in any way could only expect the severest retribution. Josephus declares that he was 'contemptuous of justice'.[212]

He was totally devoted to his Idumaean family, his parents, brothers and his sister. He avenged the death of his father and his brother Joseph, and was particularly attached until his dying day to his sister Salome. By contrast, he often showed himself patently and atrociously cruel to his in-laws. Hyrcanus, his wife's grandfather, Alexandra, his mother-in-law, his brother-in-law, Aristobulus, and his beloved wife, Mariamme, all fell foul of his suspicious and brutal temperament. He was never able wholly to overcome his inferiority complex, stemming from his lower social status compared to that of his royal spouse, Mariamme, and the members of her family. Worst of all, he was responsible for the execution of his two Hasmonaean sons, Alexander and Aristobulus.

Outside the family circle, he knew how to please or placate those above him: the High Priest/ethnarch Hyrcanus, Julius Caesar, Mark Antony and above all Caesar Augustus in the last period of his life. In consequence, he earned the trust and respect of the Romans and rose to the dignity of client king (*rex socius*).[213] However, during his last years, after witnessing his cruelty towards Mariamme's children, Caesar Augustus saw through him and, snidely alluding to his well-known Jewish dietary habits, apparently declared: 'It is better to be Herod's pig than his son'.[214]

Josephus portrays him as an individual seemingly afflicted by schizophrenia:

Herod's policies were characterized by two distinct tendencies, a fact that usually caused surprise. On the one hand, when we have regard to his liberality and the benefactions that he had made to mankind in general, even his detractors would be forced to admit the remarkable generosity of his nature. Yet when we consider his unjustified and vengeful treatment of his subjects and his closest relatives, and observe the unrelenting harshness of his character, we must regard him as a brute . . .[215]

More than once he displayed signs resembling madness. After ordering the execution of his wife, he went on instructing his servants to call her. Later he fantasized that his son, with sword in hand, was rushing towards him with the intention of killing him. Such sick thoughts dominated him sometimes for days. His insanity culminated in the truly atrocious scenario he planned for his exit from this world. He sought to trigger an all-pervading countrywide performance of songs of lamentation through the murder of the imprisoned dignitaries of Judaea.

Again Josephus is our best-informed witness. In judging Herod, he tried to generalize, and maintained that a single common motivation explained all the actions of his split personality. His overarching desire was always to please everybody because selfishly and constantly he wanted to be admired and cherished by all:

'Herod loved honour, and was dominated by that passion, and his magnanimity revealed itself wherever there was hope of a lasting memorial or of immediate fame.'[216]

He was a man of indiscriminate cruelty, with an ungovernable temper and a contempt of justice, yet fortune favoured him as much as any man. Born a commoner, he rose to become king, and though beset by innumerable dangers he contrived to escape them all and lived to a great age. In his domestic life and relations with his sons he considered himself very fortunate for his success in defeating those he judged to be his enemies, but in my opinion this was his great misfortune.[217]

His lavish building projects were also similarly inspired:

His overriding aim was to glorify himself and his ambition was to leave to posterity ever more imposing monuments of his reign; and this was the spur that drove him to build cities and lavish such enormous expense on the work.[218]

Josephus depicts not one Herod, but two.

Evaluation of Herod's positive and negative achievements

Herod's blemishes were balanced by admirable positive qualities. Loyalty was one of his incontestable virtues. He never rebelled against the helpless and vulnerable Hasmonaean High Priest, Hyrcanus; through thick and thin, he remained, even after his defeat at Actium, a devoted friend of Mark Antony, and once he vowed allegiance to Octavian/Augustus as a client king, to the end of his life he showed himself steadfastly faithful to him.

It cannot be doubted that by virtue of his policies Judaea became a richer, more civilized and definitely more beautiful country to live in than it was before Herod was put in charge of it by the Romans. In particular, the port of Caesarea greatly contributed to the improvement of foreign trade and consequently of the economic conditions of the country and its population. Furthermore, with his great architectural projects he provided employment and improved the lifestyle of tens of thousands of the working population of Judaea.

Josephus offers another simplistic negative explanation of all the actions of Herod: in everything, including his architectural projects, he was driven by the idea of self-interest. However, this egotistical motivation cannot do full justice to his care for his subjects in need, providing not only grain for the hungry during the famine, but even bakers to cater for the elderly and warm clothing during the winter.[219] However, the extreme generosity he displayed towards the famished and the financially oppressed are not be attributed to an expectation of admiration and gratitude. At least from time to time he must have had a heart of flesh and not always a heart of stone. And when no further favour could be expected in return, with almost both his feet in the grave, why would Herod leave ten million silver coins as well as gold and silver vessels and luxurious articles of clothing to Augustus, and five million pieces of silver to the Empress Livia? To allow one to see these legacies in proportion, his bequest to his beloved sister Salome was five hundred thousand silver coins, one tenth of his gift to Livia and one twentieth of that to Augustus.[220]

On the other hand, Josephus hits the nail on the head when he points out that Herod's oft-repeated open-handedness had no sound economic basis. He frequently spent far beyond his means on his enterprises and on his patrons and friends, whether by distributing food to the needy after the famine, or on good causes at home and abroad, and even on remitting taxes when his subjects had to struggle through various financial crises. The consequences can easily be imagined:

His lavish expenditure on the recipients of his bounty made him a source of misery to the people from whom he took the money. Well aware that he was hated for the injustices . . . he could see no easy way to redress these wrongs . . . Instead he remained defiant, using the resentment (of the exploited) as an excuse to satisfy his wants.[221]

Need for funds could prevail against his openly displayed Jewish piety. Having overspent on various enterprises at home and abroad, he did not disdain the idea of filling his coffers with money gained through sacrilege. In this, he found an excuse in the precedent reported about the Hasmonaean High Priestly ruler, John Hyrcanus I.[222] Taking every precaution to be unobserved at night, like Hyrcanus before him, Herod entered the tomb of King David with some trusted companions on a treasure hunt. He was told that Hyrcanus had removed from the grave three thousand talents of silver. Herod did not have such luck, but he still discovered and had taken away a good many gold ornaments and other valuables. Superstitious fear apparently stopped further investigation close to the coffins of David and Solomon. Two of Herod's bodyguards are said to have been struck dead. So the exploration was discontinued and to placate the spiritual powers, Herod erected an expensive marble monument at the entrance of the tomb. Nicolas of Damascus mentions the monument, but thinks it wiser to keep silent on the desecration of the tomb of David by Herod that lay behind it.[223]

The basic insecurity inflicted on Herod by the knowledge that Mariamme and her family despised him, produced a constant longing for flattery. Sycophancy was always welcome, but even the slightest questioning of his authority opened the floodgates of reprisals. Hence Josephus concludes:

These excesses he committed from a desire to be uniquely honored. To support my contention that this was his overriding motive I can refer to the ways in which he gave honour to Caesar, Agrippa and his other friends. He expected to receive the same deference himself as he showed to his superiors … The Jewish people, however, have been taught by their Law … to admire righteousness rather than the pursuit of glory. As a result, they incurred his displeasure, finding it impossible to flatter the king's ambition with statues, temples and marks of honour.[224]

To end on a positive note, it is important to draw attention to Herod's contribution to the religious life of his country. Herod's fondness of the learned Pharisees and of the Essenes, these prophetic experts in divine mysteries,[225] identified by many with the members of the sect who owned the Qumran or Dead Sea Scrolls, was bound to advance and promote the intellectual and spiritual life of the Jewish people.

Above all, the rebuilding of the Temple instilled a fresh life and a much increased attractiveness into Jewish worship and surely enlarged the number of the Jewish pilgrims and the non-Jewish tourists who visited Jerusalem throughout the years. The pilgrims came from the four corners of the ancient world, even from beyond the

Figure 7.1 *Qumran and the Dead Sea.*

borders of the Roman Empire. According to the Acts of the Apostles, the Jewish crowds present in Jerusalem at the pilgrim-feast of Shabuot or Feast of Weeks, the first Christian Pentecost, who were addressed by St Peter, came from Parthia, Media, Elam, Mesopotamia, Cappadocia, Pontus, Asia, Phrygia, Pamphilia, Egypt, Cyrene, Rome, Crete and Arabia. The Jerusalem sanctuary was one of the marvels of the ancient world. According to a Jewish proverbial saying preserved in the Babylonian Talmud, 'He who has not seen the Temple of Herod has not seen a beautiful building in his life'.[226]

So how can one sum up the variegated pictures of Herod? Let us look at two extreme views expressed by contemporary historians. At the one end, a somewhat rash Josephus expert, Professor Steve Mason, formerly of MacMaster University in Canada and now at Aberdeen University, calls Herod an 'infamous king'.[227] Such an assessment is

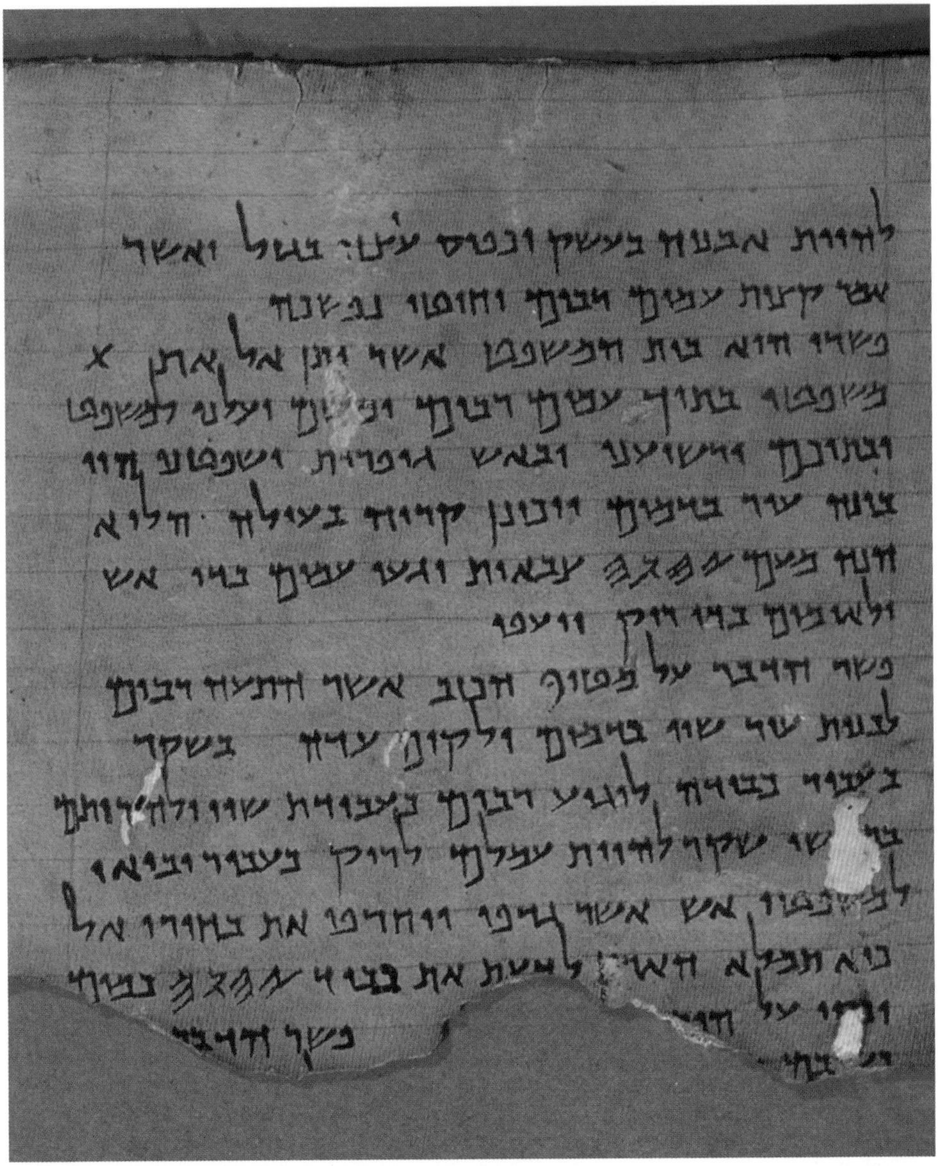

Figure 7.2 *The Habakkuk Commentary from Qumran.*

Figure 7.3 *The beginning of the Community Rule from Qumran.*

exclusively based on the negative aspects of Herod's character and behaviour, especially towards his own family, but bypasses his remarkable political and economic achievements, his acts of genuine generosity and his creation of architectural masterpieces.[228]

At the other end, A.H.M. Jones believes that Herod truly earned the epithet 'the Great': 'His aim was at bottom, sane and enlightened, and if they could have learnt from him the Jews would have been saved much suffering'.[229] In the eyes of Abraham Schalit, a perspicacious and profoundly learned twentieth-century student of the Herodian age, Herod was a genuine hero with a wise statesman's penetrating vision. He sought to promote the wellbeing of the Jewish people, but his good works were often frustrated by the frightening flaws of his personality.[230] In turn, Ernst Baltrusch, in his excellent recent monograph, stresses Herod's outstanding position on the world scene. He was literally 'the Third Man' in the Roman Empire, standing immediately after Augustus and his greatest friend, Agrippa.[231] He dreamt of an unprecedented uplift of the social, cultural and economic status of the Jews. He showered genuine love and care on them when they suffered, and longed for this love to be fully and continuously reciprocated. Moreover, since the Roman Empire represented for him a divinely instituted new world, and the Emperor Augustus the universal saviour of civilized humanity, Herod was determined to ensure that he did everything he could to make his Jewish kingdom an integral and significant part of this novel order.

Alas, his great dream collapsed for two reasons. For the Jews, the Roman Empire was not the new creation dreamt of by their prophets, nor was for them Augustus the final redeemer. They preferred to wait for their own royal Messiah and for the Kingdom of God, which this Messiah was to inaugurate. Moreover, the bloodbath inflicted by Herod on the much respected and loved Hasmonaean royal family, including his adored wife and favourite sons, cast a dark shadow on his generosity and good intentions towards the Jewish nation. Fate caught up with the erring tyrant and his fall, like that of all tragic heroes, proved inevitable.[232] In the Christian world, his persistent ill repute is founded on the massacre of the innocents, a crime which he never committed. However, having murdered his nearest and dearest, after a horrendously painful illness he expired in loneliness, with even his closest confidante, his sister, refusing to implement his last crazy will.

Herod in literature and cinema

After the well-known and highly popular medieval mystery plays of the fifteenth century, the dramatic potential of the figure of Herod continued to be explored in the domain of the theatre, music and cinema over the centuries, with interest being mainly focused on Herod's ill-fated marriage to Mariamme. It produced a number of novels and plays as well as an opera and a ballet between the sixteenth and twentieth centuries, including *Mariamne* by Voltaire (1725), *Herodes und Mariamne* by the German dramatist Christian Friedrich Hebbel (1850) and *Herod and Mariamne* by the Nobel Prize winning Swedish author, Pär Lagerquist (1967). Oddly, I am aware only of one full-length feature film on Herod, an unfortunately wholly predictable and rather mediocre Italian/American co-production, *Erode il Grande/Herod the Great*, made in 1958 and directed by Arnaldo Genoino, with Edmond Purdom playing Herod and Sylvia Lopez as Mariamme.

It is truly a great pity that it never occurred to William Shakespeare to add a Tragedy of King Herod of Jewry to his *Julius Caesar* and *Antony and Cleopatra*. However, as the Bard saw him, Herod was not a suitable character for the role of a tragic hero. The Herod of Shakespeare was a mixture of the bloodthirsty baby murderer of the Gospel of Matthew and the ridiculous and detestable character of the ranting, raving king of the medieval mystery plays. All the same, there are incidental allusions in two of the Shakespearean plays, *Antony and Cleopatra* and *Hamlet*, which whet one's appetite. Who but Shakespeare could think of putting words such as these on the lips of Charmian, Cleopatra's friend, in *Antony and Cleopatra* III. 3:

Let me be married to three kings in a forenoon, and widow them all: let me have a child at fifty, to whom Herod of Jewry may do homage.

Note the menacing undertone: we know what happens to babes whom Herod proposes to 'worship'.[233] And remember the hilarious warning given by Hamlet (III.2) to actors not to allow themselves to overplay violent characters: they must not '*out-herod Herod*'. The splendid Shakespearean neologism is inspired by the ridiculous figure of the mystery plays.

The only Shakespeare passage which cannot easily be explained by means of the Gospel of Matthew and/or from the Christian tradition that derived from it, is the dialogue between Alexas and the Egyptian queen in *Antony and Cleopatra* (I. 2):

ALEXAS: Good majesty, Herod of Jewry dare not look upon you but when you are well pleased.

CLEOPATRA: That Herod's head I'll have: but how, when Antony is gone through whom I might command it?

It has been suggested that since beheading is mentioned, the Herod referred to must be, not Herod the Great, but his son Herod Antipas, the tetrarch of Galilee, who ordered the decapitation of John the Baptist.[234] But the confusion theory is totally groundless. Cleopatra obviously envisages the taking of the head of a Herod who was her contemporary.[235] From reading the Gospels, Shakespeare would have known the John the Baptist episode happened a hundred years after Cleopatra's suicide. A better explanation is needed. Here is an attempt to supply one.

Since the conflict between Cleopatra and Herod is not echoed either in the New Testament or in Plutarch, the main source of Roman history for Shakespeare available for him in Thomas North's English translation since 1579, he must have discovered it somewhere else. Could the lines in *Antony and Cleopatra* depend, directly or indirectly, on Josephus?[236] The theory seems not to have been aired so far, but it is not without foundation.

The Josephus expert, Professor Tessa Rajak, reminds me that the printed Latin translation of Josephus circulated in Europe since 1470 and, what is more significant, an English rendering of the *Famous and Memorable Works of Josephus, a Man of much Honour and Learning among the Jews*, was published by Thomas Lodge, 'Doctor in Physick', in London in 1602, four to five years before the completion of *Antony and Cleopatra* in 1606/7. So it was possible for Shakespeare to find his inspiration in Josephus's account of Cleopatra and Herod.

Can anyone come up with a more plausible suggestion?

Part Three

The descendants of Herod in the New Testament and Josephus

Introduction

The picture of Herod the Great would be incomplete without a further investigation of his and his family's impact on Jewish history as well as on the history of Jesus and early Palestinian Christianity. The coexistence between Herod and Jesus, brief though it was, amounting to a maximum of a couple of years, but possibly only to a few months, enabled the evangelist Matthew to create the stories of the murder of the infants of Bethlehem and the escape of Joseph, Mary and the newborn child to Egypt.[237]

When manipulative Herod discovered the failure of his stratagem – the magi, whom he tried to use as informers regarding the whereabouts of the newborn king, fled Judaea without reporting to him – he dispatched his soldiers with the order to kill all male infants in the Bethlehem region. The story of the massacre of the innocents was taken literally for more than 1,700 years, when the whole narrative relating to the birth of Jesus was treated as Gospel truth. Church-inspired credulity was further reinforced by the historical evidence with regard to Herod's savagery towards his own sons. However, the anecdote of the killing of the little boys of Bethlehem, which has inspired many a gruesomely splendid medieval artistic creation, can hardly be taken for solid facts of history.

In Matthew's presentation of Herod's murder plot, the main dramatic element is missing as the solution comes before the problem. We know in advance that Jesus would escape as Joseph is forewarned of the approaching danger and immediately takes evasive steps by fleeing in good time to neighbouring Egypt. Egypt provides the clue to the complex. The escape of the family from menacing Herod to the land of the Nile is the

Figure I.1 Massacre of the Innocents *by Giotto di Bondone (c.1266–1337) Fresco in the Arena Chapel, Padua, Italy.*

counter-image of the exodus of the Jews under the leadership of Moses from murderous and oppressive Pharaoh, first to the desert of Sinai and ultimately to the Holy Land.

Although the savagery reflected in the decree of extermination pronounced on the Bethlehem infants is consonant with the character of the Herod of history, we have good reasons to assume that the murder plot derives from a theme solidly embedded in an ancient Jewish midrash, the popular understanding of the biblical narrative in the age of Jesus and during the subsequent early rabbinic period. The story told in the Old Testament book of Exodus in which the king of Egypt decides to destroy all the newborn

Figure I.2 *The flight to Egypt shown in a woodcut by Albrecht Dürer, from his 'Life of the Virgin' series published in 1511.*

Jewish boys, including Moses, inspires Matthew's narration concerning Herod's wicked design aimed at the elimination of Jesus. Post-biblical Jewish literature, represented by Josephus, the anonymous first-century CE writer designated as Pseudo-Philo and the ancient rabbis, recounts how the father and mother of Moses were informed in advance of their son's destiny.

According to the Bible, Pharaoh decreed that all the newborn male Jewish children were to be drowned in the Nile. By reducing the number of the Israelite slaves, he intended to ensure that they would never constitute a real threat to Egyptian survival. All the other Jewish babes perished in the river, but Moses, placed by his parents in a reed basket, escaped drowning and was brought to safety by Pharaoh's daughter, who found him when she was taking a bath in the river.

Figure I.3 *Moses saved by Pharaoh's daughter, from the third century synagogue at Dura Europos. The Greek style of the paintings at Dura Europos is remarkable.*

By the time of Matthew, the story evolved considerably. The first century CE Pseudo-Philo, author of the *Book of Biblical Antiquities*, made the elder sister of Moses, the prophetess Miriam, disclose in advance to her parents that Moses would become the saviour of the Jews and the destroyer of Egypt:

Figure I.4 Moses Saved from the Water *by Raphael, 1519, Palazzi Pontifici, Vatican.*

And the spirit of God came upon Maria by night, and she saw a dream, and told her parents in the morning, saying: I saw this night, and behold a man in a linen garment stood and said to me: Go and tell your parents; behold that which shall be born of you shall be cast into the water, for by him water shall be dried up, and by him will I do signs, and I will save my people, and he shall have the captaincy of them always.[238]

This story was later echoed by the rabbis, too.[239] Josephus, a contemporary of both Matthew and Pseudo-Philo, outdid the latter by bringing to the notice of Pharaoh, the antitype of Herod, the future redeeming role of a Jewish boy, Moses, who would rescue the Jews and inflict harm on the Egyptians. Such a premonition inspired Pharaoh's decision to exterminate all the male Jewish infants of that age in order to eliminate

Moses, the unidentified future saviour of the Jews. An Egyptian scribe, expert in their sacred books, plays the role of Herod's Bible interpreting chief priests, and notifies Pharaoh of the impending birth of a Jewish boy who, if allowed to live, would become the nemesis of Egypt:

One of the sacred scribes – persons with considerable skill in accurately predicting the future – announced to the king that there would be born to the Israelites at that time one who would abase the sovereignty of the Egyptians and exalt the Israelites, were he reared to manhood, and would surpass all men in virtue and win everlasting renown. Alarmed thereat, the king, on this sage's advice, ordered that every male child born to the Israelites should be destroyed by being cast into the river, and that the labours of Hebrew women with child should be observed by Egyptian midwives ... But no man can defeat the will of God ... For this child, whose birth the sacred scribe foretold, was reared, eluding the king's vigilance, and the prophet's words concerning all that was to be wrought through him proved true ...[240]

The tradition preserved in rabbinic literature is parallel to the one found in Josephus and is likely to be equally old (first century CE). There too the revelation of a threat to the life of the baby Moses is associated with a dream, except that the visionary is not the friendly sister of Moses, but the arch-enemy of the Jews, Pharaoh himself. In his dream, recounted in Aramaic, the king of Egypt saw a balance. All the Egyptians were placed in one of its scales and a 'lamb (*talya*), the little one of a ewe', stood in the other, but amazingly it weighed more than the whole of Egypt. The puzzled Pharaoh immediately summoned all the magicians of Egypt (the magi of Matthew) and revealed to them his night vision. Their leaders, Yanis and Yimbres, corresponding to the Jannes and Jambres of the New Testament[241] or to Jannes and his brother of the Damascus Document from the Dead Sea Scrolls,[242] had no difficulty in solving the mystery. The word *talya* furnished the clue with is double meaning of lamb and boy (not unlike the English kid capable of designating the young of a goat or a child). So they declared to Pharaoh: 'A boy is about to be born in the congregation of Israel by whose hand the whole land of Egypt will be destroyed.'[243]

Pharaoh knew what to do to deal effectively with this peril. Here is then the prototype of Herod's massacre of the innocents whose source is more likely to be Jewish folklore than genuine history.

Jesus and other New Testament figures, such as John the Baptist, the apostle James, son of Zebedee, and St Paul were bound to cross the path of Herod's descendants, who played a significant role in the life of Palestinian Jewry during the first seven decades of the first century CE. As will be shown, the tetrarch of Galilee, Herod Antipas, was in particular involved with Jesus and John the Baptist, King Agrippa I ordered the execution of James, the son of Zebedee, and Agrippa II conversed with St Paul in Caesarea. In the following brief survey an attempt will be made to recount the impact of the Herodians on late Second Temple Judaism and nascent Christianity.

8

Herod Archelaus (4 BCE–6 CE)[244]

The accession of Archelaus, Herod's son by the Samaritan wife, Malthace, and successor to the rulership (*ethnarchy*) of Judaea (4 BCE–6 CE), is used in Matthew's Gospel to explain the decision of the parents of Jesus to settle in Nazareth, in the northern province of Galilee, on their return from their escape to Egypt. Previously Matthew assumes that they lived in Bethlehem in Judaea. The evangelist takes it for granted that this move to the more distant province was necessary because a son was imagined to be as dangerous as his father. The argument is hollow, however, since Galilee, too, was governed throughout the whole lifetime of Jesus by another son of Herod, Antipas. Luke needed no justification for the journey; the family was supposed simply to return to 'their own city of' Nazareth, where they had resided before the census decree brought them to Bethlehem.[245]

Since at the end of his life Herod went on changing his will regarding his successor, choosing first Antipater, then Antipas and finally Archelaus, it is not surprising that the final nomination did not go unopposed. Archelaus's brother, Antipas, hastened to Rome and tried to unseat him, as did also other members of Herod's family. A separate delegation of anti-Herodian Jewish notables followed them to the imperial capital, and petitioned the authorities for direct Roman rule in Judaea. Revolutionary upheavals up and down the country also delayed the final settlement until peace was established by the armies of Varus, governor of Syria.[246] Meanwhile, Nicolas of Damascus quietly pulled strings in favour of Archelaus and obtained his confirmation by Augustus, but he was obliged by the Emperor to put up with the rank of *ethnarch* of Judaea, Idumaea and Samaria, less imposing than that of king, a position which he was to hold for ten years. On his coins, he appears as 'Herod the ethnarch'.

Figure 8.1 *Coin of Herod the ethnarch.*

The lawless rule of Archelaus angered both the Jews and the Samaritans, and he further displeased his traditional Jewish subjects by marrying, contrary to the stipulation of the Torah, the widow of his executed half-brother, Alexander. Charges were levelled against him before Augustus. Archelaus was allowed to speak up for himself, but the Emperor turned a deaf ear to his apologia and deposed him, confiscating all his possessions. He was exiled to Gaul. Quirinius's census followed, and Herod's kingdom of Judaea was reduced to the status of a Roman province in 6 CE.[247] The change took effect with the arrival of the first governor, Coponius (6–9 CE).[248]

Open subjugation to Rome evoked national resistance headed by Judas the Galilean and the creation of the revolutionary movement of the Zealots/Sicarii. Their clandestine or open opposition to the Roman power underlay Jewish history in the Holy Land during the following decades and culminated in the great and catastrophic revolt, which saw the end of the Jewish political entity in 70 CE.[249]

9

Herod Antipas (4 BCE–39 CE)[250]

Antipas, the second son of Herod the Great also by Malthace, is the most frequently mentioned Herodian personality in the New Testament. He had dealings with both Jesus and John the Baptist. His name appears no fewer than twenty-four times in the Synoptic Gospels and the Acts of the Apostles. He is referred to either as tetrarch or more incorrectly as king.[251] He called himself simply Herod on his coins, a style attested also in the New Testament. His real name, 'Antipas', is known only from Josephus. In 20 CE, he moved his capital to the newly founded city of Tiberias, named in honour of the Emperor Tiberius and built on the shore of the Lake of Galilee.

Figure 9.1 *Coin of Herod the tetrarch from Tiberias.*

Figure 9.2 *Coin of Queen Salome.*

Antipas ruled over both Galilee and Peraea in Transjordan. He was first married to the daughter of the Nabataean king Aretas IV,[252] but divorced her when he fell in love with Herodias, his sister-in-law, the wife of his half-brother Herod. She was the daughter of Aristobulus, Mariamme's executed son, and the mother of the 'dancing girl', Salome, who later became the wife of Philip, Antipas's brother, and afterwards married King Aristobulus of Chalcis. The Herodians face us with truly amazing marital complexities.

The humiliated Nabataean wife of Antipas fled to Petra, passing through the mountain-top fortress of Machaerus, and her father, Aretas IV, set out with his army to avenge her humiliation and inflicted a severe defeat on the forces of his son-in-law.

The matrimonial episode provides the New Testament link with John the Baptist. Having openly voiced, according to the Gospels, his disapproval of Antipas's remarriage, the Baptist got into Herodias's bad books.[253] Opportunity for retribution arose when, at his birthday celebration, attended by all his courtiers and the notables of Galilee, Antipas was so pleased with the dance performance of Herodias's daughter Salome, that he rashly promised her anything she cared to ask him. On her mother's advice, Salome demanded and received on a platter the head of John. According to Josephus, the defeat of Antipas's army by the Nabataeans was the divine retribution for the Baptist's murder.[254]

In the version handed down by Josephus, the Baptist's downfall is attributed, not to his criticism and condemnation of Antipas's marriage, but to his eloquence, which the

Figure 9.3 *Salome dancing at Herod's Banquet, by Fra Filippo Lippi, 1464.*

Figure 9.4 Salome with the head of John the Baptist, *by Titian, c. 1550.*

tetrarch considered ominous as with his fiery preaching he was capable of inciting the people to rebellion:

Herod put him [John the Baptist] to death, though he was a good man and had exhorted the Jews to lead righteous lives … and so doing join in baptism … When others too joined the crowds about him, because they were aroused to the highest degree by his sermons, Herod became alarmed. Eloquence that had so great an effect on mankind might lead to some form of sedition … Herod decided therefore

Figure 9.5 *The so-called Mona Lisa Mosaic from Sepphoris. It appears on the floor of a large dining room near the summit of the site, in what was most probably the house of an important gentile. The richly adorned figure of the mosaic has become known as the 'Mona Lisa of Galilee'.*

Figure 9.6 *The signs of the Zodiac. This mosaic floor is in the Hammat-Tiberias synagogue. The central panel represents a zodiac wheel, with the four seasons in each corner, and the sun or Helios in the centre.*

that it would be much better to strike first and be rid of him before his work led to an uprising.[255]

This is why he was taken to Machaerus and beheaded. In Josephus, there is no mention of a birthday party, nor of Salome's dance. Distant Machaerus would have been an unlikely venue for a family celebration to be attended by all the Galilean aristocracy. In fact, as has already been mentioned, Josephus alludes to the rumour circulating among the Jews that the defeat of Antipas's army by the Nabataeans was a divine vengeance instigated by the murder of the Baptist.[256]

Having inherited the enthusiasm of Herod his father for monumental architecture, Antipas distinguished himself by restoring the city of Sepphoris, destroyed by

Varus during his campaign against Galilean rebels after the death of Herod the Great in 4 BCE.[257] He made it his capital and turned it into 'the ornament of Galilee'.[258] Although it lies only four miles north of Nazareth, curiously it is never mentioned in the Gospels.

Antipas also erected a splendid new capital, replacing Sepphoris, by the Lake of Galilee. It was named Tiberias and organized as a Greek city. It had a palace with animal decorations and a theatre, but also an imposing synagogue. Unmentioned in the Synoptic Gospels, it figures in John.[259] John also designates the Lake of Galilee as the Sea of Tiberias.[260]

Like his father, Antipas avoided putting human effigies on his coins, and according to the testimony of Luke, he went on a Passover pilgrimage to Jerusalem where he came

Figure 9.7 *Bust of Gaius Caligula, held in the Metropolitan Museum of Art, New York.*

into contact with Jesus in the course of his trial by Pilate.[261] If we are to believe the same Luke, Antipas had a superstitious fear of Jesus whom he thought to be the reincarnation of the executed John the Baptist.[262] According to one tradition, he was curious to meet him, but according to another, he was planning to kill Jesus, who disparagingly referred to him as a fox.[263]

Still following Luke, there was a dramatic encounter between Jesus and Herod Antipas in Jerusalem. When Pilate learnt that Jesus was from Galilee, he decided to send the accused man to be judged by the ruler of his own province. However, disappointed and angered by the unwillingness of Jesus to entertain him with a miracle, he dispatched him back to Pilate and the cross.[264]

Made jealous by the award of the royal title to his nephew, Agrippa I, a friend of the new Emperor, a title which was denied to him, Antipas appealed to Gaius Caligula (37–41 CE) for equal promotion. But his envoy to Rome betrayed him and accused him of treason. Consequently Antipas was demoted from his office of tetrarch, and like his brother Archelaus before him, he was exiled to Gaul, to Lugdunum (Lyons), where he died, possibly assassinated by order of Caligula, who liked to get rid of out-of-favour dignitaries.[265]

10

Herod Philip
(4 BCE–33/4 CE)

The son of Herod the Great and his wife Cleopatra of Jerusalem was allotted after the death of his father the area lying north-east and east of Galilee (Batanaea, Auranitis, Paneas, etc.), territories which were inhabited by Greeks and Syrians. No hostile comment is attached to his name either in Josephus or in the New Testament. Luke merely states that in the fifteenth year of Tiberius (28/9 CE), when John the Baptist appeared on the public scene, Philip was the ruler of Ituraea and Trachonitis.[266] He called himself Philip the Tetrarch, without Herod, on his coins.

Like his father, he too was a great builder. He renovated and beautified the fishing village of Bethsaida, the place of origin of the apostles Peter, Andrew and Philip, and dedicated the new town to Livia, the widow of Augustus, and renamed it Julias.[267] According to Josephus, he died there in the twentieth year of Tiberius (33/34 CE) and was buried in a tomb he had prepared for himself.[268]

Philip also reconstructed Paneas or Banias, at the sources of the Jordan and called it Caesarea in honour of Augustus. This is Philip's Caesarea or Caesarea Philippi of the Gospels, distinguished from the port city of Palestine or Caesarea Maritima.[269] He was the first husband of Salome, the notorious daughter of Herodias, herself the second wife of Herod Antipas. Philip was a very approachable person and renowned for his love of justice. His servants always carried a judgement seat so that he could hear cases and pronounce sentence wherever he was asked to do so.[270]

Figure 10.1 *Caesarea Philippi.* The niches held statues dedicated to the Greek god Pan and are part of a religious complex built at one of the sources of the Jordan River.

Figure 10.2 *Coin of Herod Philip with the effigy of Tiberius.*

As Philip ruled over a non-Jewish population, he minted coins bearing the effigies of the Emperor (Augustus and Tiberius) and even his own. On his death, his domain was attached for a short while to the Roman province of Syria and was later transferred to Agrippa I in 37 BCE.

11

Herod Agrippa I
(41–44 CE)[271]

Agrippa was Herod the Great's grandson. His father was Aristobulus, Mariamme's executed son, and his mother, Berenice, was the daughter of Herod's sister, Salome, and her executed second husband, Costabar. Born in 10 BCE, he was sent for education at the age of six to the imperial capital, and he remained there and led the adventurous life of a spendthrift for more than a quarter of a century. To keep up with his friend, Drusus, the son of the Emperor Tiberius, he accumulated enormous debts, and when the death of Drusus deprived him from protection, pressure from the creditors compelled him to run away from Rome. His sister, Herodias, by then wife of Herod Antipas, received him and he was appointed supervisor of the market in Tiberias. He soon quarrelled with Antipas and lost his job, and was forced to take refuge with an old friend from Rome, Flaccus, by then governor of Syria. It did not take long for Flaccus to discover Agrippa's dishonesty, but he somehow managed to escape to Italy in 36 CE. He was welcomed by the Emperor Tiberius in Capri, who lent him a large sum of money, a loan that he repaid by incurring a further debt with the mother of the future Emperor Claudius. Without delay, he got on the right side of Caligula, the great-nephew of the Emperor, and foolishly aired his hope in public that Caligula should soon replace Tiberius. This imprudence landed him in prison. But Tiberius soon died; Caligula succeeded him in 37 CE. The new Emperor released Agrippa from gaol and exchanged his chain of iron for one of the same weight in gold. He moreover appointed him to the tetrarchy of Herod Philip in Batanaea and the neighbouring regions north-east and east of Galilee, and granted him the title of king. Three years later, in 40 CE, Galilee and Peraea were added to the realm of Agrippa after the sacking and exiling of Herod Antipas.

After the assassination of Caligula in 41 CE, Agrippa was successful in engineering that his other childhood friend, Claudius, should mount the imperial throne (41–54 CE). The grateful new Emperor added Judaea and Samaria to the territories of Agrippa. From 41 to 44 CE, he ruled over a kingdom which was as large as that of Herod the Great and described himself as King Agrippa on his coins.

Figure 11.1 *Bust of Claudius, held in the British Museum.*

We have two diametrically opposite pictures and evaluations of the short reign of Agrippa I. The Jewish sources, Josephus and rabbinic literature, grant him warm approval, but he was given bad press in the Acts of the Apostles in the New Testament. Although, following in the footsteps of his grandfather, he tried to serve Judaism at home and Hellenism abroad, Jewish circles did not hold against him his pro-Hellene attitudes. In Beirut he built a theatre and an amphitheatre and organized games there as well as in Caesarea. He was called 'friend of the Emperor' and 'friend of the Romans', and while his coins struck at home displayed no human effigy, those minted abroad were decorated by the image of the Emperor or of his own. Nevertheless, the Romans were not always pleased. His building of a wall in Jerusalem was stopped and the council of six client kings convoked by him in Tiberias was disbanded by Marsus, the suspicious governor of Syria.[272]

Figure 11.2 *Coin of Agrippa I.*

The Jewish sources, by contrast, stress his devotion to Judaism. His gesture of donating the gold chain of Caligula to the Temple on his first visit made a deep impression as did also the sacrifice of thanksgiving he offered and his financial assistance to the Nazirites, thanks to which they were enabled to fulfil their vows. Agrippa personally performed the reading of the prescribed section of Deuteronomy at the ceremony of closure of the sabbatical year in 42 CE. The Pharisees approved of Agrippa's policies and, overlooking his Idumaean ancestry, they called him their brother.[273] Josephus, in turn, praised him for his regular attendance of the Temple services and his generosity towards Jews living in the diaspora. On one occasion, it is reported that Agrippa had pardoned a leading Pharisee who had criticized him for breaking the Law. Instead of punishing him, he dismissed him with a present. Josephus went even as far as to award him the title of 'great king'.[274]

A very different Agrippa emerges from the New Testament tradition, where he is depicted as a determined persecutor of the early church. Without any explanation or justification he is said to have arrested members of the Christian community and issued an order for the beheading of the apostle James, son of Zebedee. When he noticed that the Jewish population had approved of his act, he threw Peter too into prison. When with the help of an angel he miraculously escaped, in an outburst of fury, the king ordered the execution of all the guards. According to the Acts of the Apostles, a terrible death was the divine retribution for the wicked deeds of Agrippa. When robed in glorious garments, he made a speech to a delegation from Tyre and Sidon, his sycophantic entourage declared that his voice was that of a god. This sacrilegious flattery produced instant retribution; an angel appeared and struck him, and his body was immediately devoured by worms.[275] The story underlying the legend in the Acts is described by Josephus in slightly less fanciful terms. The rays of the rising sun made the shiny, silvery robes of Agrippa glitter and his honey-tongued courtiers compared him to a god. Since the king did not protest at once, after seeing the bad omen of an owl, an unbearable abdominal pain seized him. Piously he accepted that his hour had come by the will of God; he died five days later and was mourned by the entire Jewish population of his kingdom.[276]

The two portraits, the hostile Christian and the friendly Jewish, are impossible to reconcile, but on the whole the transformation of the young rascal and adventurer into a repentant and kind middle-aged man seems more probable than the abruptly nasty and violent figure presented by the New Testament.

12

Herod of Chalcis (41–48 CE)[277]

Herod of Chalcis, grandson of Herod the Great, was the brother of Agrippa I, whom Claudius appointed to rule over Ituraea and Abilene, territories lying north of Galilee. He married his niece Berenice, Agrippa's daughter, who later became the mistress of the Roman general and future Emperor, Titus. After the death of Agrippa I, he was granted the privilege by Claudius to appoint Jewish High Priests and oversee the administration of the Jerusalem Temple. On his coins he calls himself 'friend of Claudius'. His nephew, Agrippa II, was to inherit his territories. He is not mentioned in the New Testament.

Figure 12.1 *Coin of Herod of Chalcis.*

13

Herod Agrippa II (50–92/3 or 100 CE)[278]

The son of King Agrippa I, and great-grandson of Herod the Great, Agrippa II, or with his full Roman name, Marcus Julius Agrippa, was a 17-year-old student in Rome when his father died in 44 CE. The Emperor Claudius was advised not to elevate him to the kingship at once, and the young man remained in Rome to complete his education until 52 CE. His rise to rulership was progressive. In 50 CE he inherited the small kingdom of Ituraea and the supervision of the Jerusalem Temple from his uncle, Herod of Chalcis. A little later, in 53 CE, he was made the ruler of Herod Philip's tetrarchy of Batanaea, Gaulanitis and Trachonitis together with part of Galilee, including the cities of Tiberias, Tarichaeae and Julias on the lake shore. However, he was not put in charge of most of the Holy Land, the government of which between 44 and 66 CE remained in the hands of Roman procurators. He was a devoted servant of his Roman masters and assisted them with troops in 54 CE in the war against the Parthians. In 60 CE, he led the welcoming party on the arrival of Porcius Festus, the new governor of Judaea. To court the favours of the Emperor Nero, he changed the name of his capital Caesarea Philippi to Neronias. On his coins he calls himself King Agrippa.

Agrippa II was greatly devoted to his Jewish subjects and looked after their wellbeing. To save them from unemployment, he re-engaged the 18,000 building workers after the completion of their labour on Herod's Temple under the procurator

Figure 13.1 *Coin of Agrippa II with Vespasian's head on one side and Agrippa's name on the other.*

Figure 13.2 *Bust of Nero.*

Albinus (62–4 CE) and employed them to pave the streets of Jerusalem with white stones. He observed the laws of Judaism, and was often engaged in discussion with rabbis. In particular, he ensured that the non-Jewish husbands of his sister Berenice underwent circumcision.

In 66 CE, at the outbreak of the great rebellion, Agrippa supported the peace party of the Jewish aristocrats, but when the insurgents carried the day, he turned his back on them and openly sided with the Romans. In 67 CE, he welcomed Vespasian, the general of the Roman forces in Caesarea Philippi, and the next year, after Nero's suicide, he travelled to Rome with Vespasian's son, Titus, before being summoned back by Berenice on learning that the Roman armies of the east had proclaimed Vespasian Emperor in 69 CE. For the rest of the war and during the whole siege of Jerusalem, Agrippa stood all the time by Titus, the new Roman commander-in-chief. He was rewarded for his steadfast support with further territories in Lebanon. In 75 CE, we find him in Rome, where he was elevated to the rank of praetor.

He was in constant contact with Josephus and wrote to him sixty-two letters. In one of these, quoted by the historian, Agrippa showered praises on Josephus's *Jewish War*, which he qualified to be the best among all the accounts of the conflict, and asked him for the remaining volumes.[279] Elsewhere Josephus reports that, instead of sending him complimentary copies, he sold the whole work to 'the most admirable King Agrippa'.[280]

Before recounting the encounter of Agrippa and his sister with St Paul, a few words need to be written about Berenice. She was another of the *femmes fatales* of antiquity whose activities filled the gossip columns of the Roman world. She was three times married. Her first husband was Marcus Julius Alexander, the Romanized son of the famous Alexandrian Jewish financier, Alexander the Alabarch, who was the brother of the philosopher Philo of Alexandria. Marcus, in turn, was the brother of Tiberius Julius Alexander, the Roman procurator of Judaea from 46 to 48 CE and later chief of staff of the Roman army during the siege of Jerusalem. After her first husband's untimely death, Berenice became the wife of her uncle, the earlier mentioned Herod of Chalcis, to whom she bore two sons.[281] By 48 CE, when she was in her twenties, she was widowed again and joined the court of her brother Agrippa. Rumour had it both in Judaea and in

Figure 13.3 *Bust of Vespasian.*

Rome that they lived in an incestuous relation. To squash the gossip, she persuaded Polemon of Pontus, king of Cilicia, to marry her, but divorce soon followed and she was again back in the court of Agrippa.

Josephus refers to the liaison,[282] and it is also alluded to in the well-known lines of Juvenal, the Roman satirical poet, who speaks of a diamond ring, famous for being the gift of the 'barbarian' Agrippa and worn on the finger of his incestuous sister:

Deinde adamas notissimus et Beronices
in digito factus pretiosior. Hunc dedit olim
barbarus incestae dedit hunc Agrippa sorori.
Observant ubi festa mero pede sabbata reges
Et vetus indulget senibus clementia porcis.[283]

Figure 13.4 *Bust of Titus.*

Berenice's supreme conquest was Titus, Vespasian's son, who became her lover while in charge of the conduct of the war against the Jews in 69 CE when he was 30 years old and the no doubt well-preserved Berenice 50. Titus' 'passionate longing'[284] for her prompted him to return quickly to Judaea from Rome, where he had been sent by his father. He had been instructed to spy out the lie of the land in the early days of the vacancy of the imperial throne after Nero had committed suicide in 68 CE. In 75 CE Berenice was still openly living with Titus in Rome as his mistress, and the gossipmongers of the capital prognosticated an impending wedding as she was already behaving as Titus's wife.[285] The affair was terminated in 79 CE, when Titus was due to occupy the throne of the deceased Vespasian. Realizing that Roman public opinion would not tolerate his marriage to Berenice, he brought himself to dismiss her 'against his will and hers' ('invitus invitam', in the words of Suetonius). Their tragic story inspired dramas by Jean

Racine and Pierre Corneille in seventeenth-century France,[286] and several Italian operas in the seventeenth and eighteenth centuries.[287]

Both Agrippa II and Berenice found their way into the New Testament. The episode, recorded in the Acts of the Apostles, is set in Caesarea where Agrippa, accompanied by his sister, the officers of his army and Jewish notables, arrived to visit the newly appointed Roman governor Porcius Festus. Festus was busy with the case of St Paul, held in Roman custody, whom the Jewish authorities of Jerusalem wanted to try on a capital charge, but Paul, using his right as a Roman citizen, prevented his handing over to the Jerusalem court by appealing for his case to be heard instead by the imperial tribunal in Rome. Having to write a report to the Emperor, but at a loss with the complexities of Jewish law and religion, Festus requested the help of Agrippa who, he thought, would understand these matters much better than he. Apparently next day, Agrippa, Berenice and their whole entourage turned up and listened to Paul's lengthy apologia. In the account of the Acts Festus lightheartedly reacted: 'You are out of your mind, Paul! Too much learning is driving you insane!' and Agrippa, when challenged by Paul to say whether he believed in the prophets, with royal imperturbability, and no doubt with an ironic smile on his face, put an end to the conversation by saying that if he carried on like this, Paul might convert even him to Christianity.[288] The king, his sister, the governor Porcius Festus and the other dignitaries abruptly left, with Agrippa apparently remarking that to him Paul seemed innocent and might have been released if he had not appealed to Caesar.

Conclusion

With the end of the Jewish state and the Herodian dynasty, and especially after the destruction of Herod's masterpiece, the Jerusalem Temple, in 70 CE, the glory that surrounded his name speedily faded away. He was already vilified in the pseudepigraphic work of the Assumption of Moses, probably dating to the beginning of the first century CE, where Herod is portrayed as a rash and perverse king:

'A wanton king, not of a priestly family, will follow ... He will be a man rash and perverse ... and for 34 years he will impose judgement on them ...'[289]

Herod's echo in rabbinic literature is also mostly negative. Instead of being celebrated as a new David, he was denigrated as a murderer, 'the wicked slave of the Hasmonaean kings'.[290] As for the Nativity stories of the New Testament, which have perpetuated Herod's darkened memory in the Christian world, they have turned him into the prototype of iniquity.[291] It was easy to metamorphose a man infamous for the killing of three of his own sons into an ogre massacring the innocent babes of Bethlehem, who intended but failed to extinguish the budding life of the child who was to become Christianity's Son of God.

The Herodian dynasty founded by him continued to remain active throughout the first century CE, but while Herod was a star, his descendants, politically mostly second-rate potentates, played only subsidiary roles in the drama without matching in power, style and grandeur the magisterial creator of the line. Despite their personal and influential connections with successive Emperors from Caligula to Nero, none of them was capable of fulfilling the first Herod's great dream of heading a powerful Jewish kingdom with an important role to play in the life of the Roman state, but at least some of them such as the two Agrippas, and in her own way the ill-fated Berenice, played significant supporting roles and found themselves in a position to pull a string or two in the corridors of power of imperial Rome.

With the death of Titus's friend, Agrippa II, in 92/3 or 100 CE, the Herodian dynasty came to an end. In 70 CE, after the destruction of the Temple of Jerusalem and the disappearance of the main institutions of Palestinian Judaism, the Sanhedrin and the High Priesthood, the time of the Herods ran out. They promptly vanished from history. If Herod the Great, dreaming of his and his country's grandeur at home and in the Roman world, could have foreseen the future, he surely would have been struck down by a sudden heart attack.

Chronology of Herod's life and his successors

BCE

73/72 Birth of Herod, son of Antipater, Idumaean statesman and Cyprus, a Nabataean Arab noble woman.

63 Pompey conquers Jerusalem. Judaea is subjected to Rome. Hyrcanus II loses the royal title, but remains High Priest and national leader. Antipater, his ally, adviser and financial administrator.

48 Julius Caesar defeats Pompey at Pharsalus. Antipater and Herod switch allegiance to Julius Caesar and are rewarded with Roman citizenship.

47 Antipater appoints Herod governor of Galilee. Herod captures and puts to death brigands. He is summoned before the Jewish high court for executing without trial, but is released.

44 Julius Caesar murdered.

43 Herod made governor of Syria by Cassius, one of Caesar's murderers. Herod's father is poisoned.

42 Battle of Philippi. Octavian and Mark Antony defeat Brutus and Cassius.

41 Herod switches allegiance to Mark Antony.

40 Parthians invade Palestine and install Antigonus king and High Priest and take Hyrcanus II to Mesopotamia. Herod is appointed king of Judaea by Rome.

37 Herod conquers Jerusalem with Roman help. Antigonus is captured and executed. Herod dismisses his first wife Doris and her son Antipater and marries the Hasmonaean princess Mariamme, granddaughter of Hyrcanus II.

36 Hyrcanus II returns from captivity.

35 Herod's brother-in-law Aristobulus is appointed High Priest then murdered.

34 Mark Antony gives Cleopatra part of Herod's territory.

31 Octavian, Caesar's heir, defeats Antony at Actium.

30 Hyrcanus II is executed by Herod. Herod joins Octavian.

29 Herod executes his wife Mariamme.

28	Herod executes his mother-in-law Alexandra.
27	Octavian becomes Augustus.
25/24	Famine in Judea.
23/22	Herod's two sons by Mariamme I, Alexander and Aristobulus, are sent to Rome for education. The building of Caesarea starts.
20/19	Reconstruction of the Temple starts.
18/17	Herod brings home his sons from Rome.
15	Sacrifices are offered on behalf of Marcus Agrippa during his visit to Jerusalem.
13	Court intrigues orchestrated by Antipater to compromise Alexander and Aristobulus. Antipater travels to Rome.
12	Herod takes Alexander and Aristobulus to Rome to accuse them before Augustus. The Emperor reconciles father and sons.
10	The construction of Caesarea is completed.
9	Herod at war with the Nabataeans.
8/7	Alexander and Aristobulus executed on slanderous charge of high treason secretly plotted by Antipater.
6	Antipater goes to Rome.
5	Antipater returns and is arrested.
4	Antipater executed. Death of Herod.
4	Disturbances put down by Varus.

BCE–CE

4–6	Archelaus, ethnarch of Judaea.
4–33/4	Herod Philip, tetrarch of Batanaea, Gaulanitis and Paneas.
4–39	Herod Antipas, tetrarch of Galilee.

CE

41–44	Agrippa I, king of Judaea.
50–92/3	Agrippa II, king of Batanaea, Gaulanitis Trachonitis, and parts of Galilee.

Notes

1 Oxford University Press, Oxford, 1939 and many subsequent prints.

2 Ezek 38:1–12.

3 In the Book of Jubilees Chapters 8–10, mankind is divided into three groups, as children of the three sons of Noah: Shem, Cham and Japhet. On the circular map, Africa, inhabited by the children of Cham, occupies the lower left segment. Europe and Asia, the land of the sons of Japhet, appear on the top left area. The Semites are placed on the top right, with the Holy Land and Jerusalem in the centre and Paradise at the top. See P.S. Alexander, 'Notes on the "imago Mundi" of the Book of Jubilees' (*JJS* 33 1982) p. 213.

4 Jub 8:19.

5 B. Porten & Ada Yardeni, *Textbook of Aramaic Documents from Ancient Egypt* (Hebrew University, Jerusalem, Texts and Studies for Students, 1986). p. 54. Transl. S. Berrin.

6 Josephus lists the Jewish High Priests of the period starting with Jaddua (*Ant.* 11. 302), followed by his son, Onias I, and Simon the Just (*Ant.* 11. 347 and 12. 43). Next came Manasse (*Ant.* 12. 147), who preceded Onias II, son of Simon the Just (*Ant.* 12. 156–66). The son of the latter, Simon II, is mentioned not only by Josephus (*Ant.* 12. 224), but also by Jesus ben Sira (Ecclus 50: 1–23). Finally, Onias III, the son of Simon II (*Ant.* 12. 225, 237; 2 Mac 3–4), brings us to the time of Antiochus Epiphanes and the Maccabaean uprising.

7 *Ant.* 12. 154–224.

8 *Ant.* 12. 129–33.

9 On Hellenism, see in particular Martin Hengel, *Judaism and Hellenism: Studies in their Encounter in Palestine during the Early Hellenistic Period* (S.C.M., London, 1974, to be read in conjunction with Fergus Millar, 'The Background to the Maccabean Revolution: Reflections on Martin Hengel's "Judaism and Hellenism"', *JJS* 29/1, 1978) pp. 1–21. For the post-biblical period, apart from 1 and 2 Maccabees from the Apocrypha, our principal source is Flavius Josephus with indirect supplements from the Dead Sea Scrolls. The importance of Josephus cannot be overestimated. Fergus Millar goes so far as to declare Josephus's *Jewish Antiquities* 'the most significant single work written in the Roman Empire'. See 'Empire, Community and Culture, Syrians, Jews and Arabs' (*JJS* 38/2, 1987) p. 147.

10 'The Hasmoneans and the Uses of Hellenism', in *A Tribute to Geza Vermes: Essays on Jewish and Christian Literature and History* (eds P.R. Davies & R.T. White), JSOT Suppl. Ser. 100 (Sheffield Academic Press, Sheffield, 1990) p. 261.

11 CD 1:5–18.

12 2 Mac 4:12–17.

13 *Hist.* 5. 8.

14 2 Mac 4:2.

15 2 Mac 4:7–10.

16 2 Mac 4:11–17.

17 2 Mac 4:23–27; *Ant.* 12. 239.

18 2 Mac 4:27–50.

19 1 Mac 1:33–34. The same events seem to be the subject of an eschatological-apocalyptic fragment among the Dead Sea Scrolls (4Q248) published in *DJD* 36, 2000, pp. 194–200 by M. Broshi and E. Eshel.

20 Dan 11:31; 1 Mac 1:54.

21 1 Mac 1:41–51; 2 Mac 6:18–7:42.

22 1 Mac 3:1–2.

23 1 Mac 3:13–26; *Ant.* 12.289; 1 Mac 4:1–25; 2 Mac 8:12:36; *Ant.* 12. 305–12; 1 Mac 4:26–35; 2 Mac 11:1–15; *Ant.* 12. 313–25.

24 1 Mac 4:36–59; 2 Mac 10:1–8; *Ant.* 12. 316–26.

25 John 10:22.

26 1 Mac 5:9–23; *Ant.* 12. 330–4.

27 1 Mac 6:28–38; 2 Mac 13:1–17; *Ant.* 12. 369–75.

28 1 Mac 7:13.

29 See Schürer-Vermes-Millar, *History* III.1 (1986) pp. 47–8, 145–7.

30 Isa 19:18–19.

31 *War* 7. 423–32. See R. Hayward, 'The Jewish Temple at Leontopolis. A Reconsideration' (*JJS* 33, 1982, pp. 429–43); A. Wasserstein, 'Notes on the Temple of Onias in Leontopolis' (*Illinois*

Classical Studies, 1993) pp. 119–29; G. Vermes, 'The Leadership of the Qumran Community: Sons of Zadok – Priests – Congregation', in *Geschichte – Tradition – Reflexion. Festschrift für Martin Hengel zum 70. Geburtstag I*, ed. P. Schäfer (Mohr Siebeck, Tübingen, 1996) pp. 375–84.

32 1 Mac 7:39–50; 2 Mac 15:1–36; *Ant.* 12. 408–12.

33 1 Mac 8:1–32; *Ant.* 12. 414–19.

34 1 Mac 9:19–21.

35 1 Mac 10:46–50; *Ant.* 13. 58–61.

36 1 Mac 12:1–47.

37 1 Mac 12:41–53; *Ant.* 13. 188–92.

38 1 Mac 13:12–24; *Ant.* 13. 203–12. I have held since 1952 that the 'Wicked Priest', chief adversary of the 'Teacher of Righteousness' in the Dead Sea Scrolls, is Jonathan Maccabaeus, to whom the description given in the Habakkuk Commentary from Cave 1 best applies. See G. Vermes, *The Complete Dead Sea Scrolls in English* (Penguin Classics, London, 2011) pp. 61, 340–1, 513. This theory has been adopted by several leading scholars, most recently by James VanderKam in the John J. Collins Festschrift, *The 'Other' in Second Temple Judaism* (Eerdmans, Grand Rapids, 2011) p. 367.

39 *Ant.* 13. 17–2.

40 1 Mac 15:6. There is no evidence that Simon minted his own currency.

41 1 Mac 13:42.

42 1 Mac 14:41.

43 1 Mac 14:48–9.

44 See 'The Hasmoneans and the Uses of Hellenism', in *A Tribute to Geza Vermes: Essays on Jewish and Christian Literature and History* (eds P.R. Davies & R.T. White), JSOT Suppl. Ser. 100 (Sheffield Academic Press, Sheffield, 1990) p. 270.

45 *Ant.* 12. 265.

46 Several Scrolls scholars, myself included, identify Simon as one of the Wicked Priests or as the Wicked Priest. See 1 Mac 13:12–24; *Ant.* 13. 203–12. I have held since 1952 that the 'Wicked Priest', chief adversary of the 'Teacher of Righteousness' in the Dead Sea Scrolls, is Jonathan Maccabaeus, to whom the description given in the Habakkuk Commentary from Cave 1 best applies. See G. Vermes, *The Complete Dead Sea Scrolls in English* (Penguin Classics, London, 2011) pp. 61–62. This theory has been adopted by several leading scholars, most recently by James VanderKam in the John J. Collins Festschrift, *The 'Other' in Second Temple Judaism* (Eerdmans, Grand Rapids, 2011) p. 367.

47 John *Hyrcanus* I (135–04 BCE) – Judah *Aristobulus* (104–03 BCE) – *Alexander* Jannaeus
    (103–76 BCE) – Salome *Alexandra* (76–67 BCE) – Judah *Aristobulus* II (67–63 BCE) – John
    Hyrcanus II (63–40 BCE) – Mattathias *Antigonus* (40–37 BCE).

48 *Ant.*13. 282–3; tSotah 13:5; ySotah 24b; bSotah 33a.

49 *Ant.* 13. 275–81.

50 *Ant.* 13. 289.

51 *Ant.* 13. 288–98.

52 *Ant.* 13. 299–300.

53 Pseudo-Jonathan is a composition that went on being updated over the centuries, but
    Deuteronomy 33:11 is one of the numerous passages whose pre-Christian origin cannot be
    seriously doubted. See Joseph Heinemann, 'Early Halakhah in the Palestinian Targumim'
    (*JJS* 25/1, 1974) p. 116.

54 *Ant.* 14. 8–10.

55 *Ant.* 13. 255–8.

56 *Ant.* 14. 403.

57 *Ant.* 20. 240.

58 *Ant.* 13. 302–17.

59 *Ant.* 13. 319.

60 *Ant.* 13. 318.

61 *Ant.* 13. 320–3. Salome is the shortened version of Shelamzion, a name appearing also in the very
    fragmentary Historical Text C-E (4Q331–3) in the Dead Sea Scrolls, which mention also
    Hyrcanus, the priest Yohanan and Aemilius (Scaurus), one of Pompey's generals. See Vermes,
    The Complete Dead Sea Scrolls (Penguin Classics, London, 2011) pp. 405–6.

62 *Ant.* 13. 357.

63 *Ant.* 13. 393–7.

64 *Ant.* 13. 372–3.

65 *Ant.* 13. 378.

66 *Ant.* 13. 380–91. These events are alluded to in the Nahum Commentary (4Q169) in the Dead
    Sea Scrolls. The Commentary states that those who 'seek smooth things', a cryptic reference to
    the Pharisees, invited 'Demetrius, king of Greece' to 'enter Jerusalem', and that 'the furious young
    lion', Jannaeus, took his revenge and hanged them alive on the tree, meaning crucifixion. See

G. Vermes, *The Complete Dead Sea Scrolls* (Penguin Classics, London, 2011) p. 505. Hanging-crucifixion was the punishment of traitors according to the Qumran Temple Scroll 64:6–13. See Vermes, ibid., p. 218.

67 J. Naveh, 'Dated Coins of Alexander Jannaeus' (*Israel Exploration Journal* 18, 1968) pp. 20–25.

68 *Ant.* 13. 398–408.

69 *Ant.* 13. 401–4; see also bSotah 22b.

70 *Ant.* 13. 380.

71 mSanh.6:5; ySanh.23c.

72 M. Hengel, *Crucifixion* (SCM Press, London, 1977) pp. 84–5.

73 *Ant.* 14. 4–7.

74 *Ant.* 14. 21.

75 *Ant.* 14. 29–33. Aemilius's name appears in the Dead Sea Scrolls. See note 61.

76 *Ant.* 14. 41–45.

77 *Ant.* 14. 58–60.

78 *War* 1. 145–51; *Ant.* 14. 61–71.

79 *Ant.* 14. 72–73.

80 *War* 1. 153; *Ant.* 14. 73.

81 *War* 184; *Ant.* 124.

82 *War* 1. 187–94; *Ant.* 14. 127–39.

83 *Ant.* 14. 213–16, 241–61.

84 Suetonius, *Divus Iulius*, 84 in *The Twelve Caesars*. Transl. Robert Graves (Penguin Classics, London, 2003) p. 42.

85 *War* 1. 218–22; *Ant.* 14. 271–6.

86 *War*. 1. 226; *Ant.* 14. 280–4.

87 *War* 1. 248–52; *Ant.* 14. 330–36.

88 *War* 1. 256–67; *Ant.* 14. 343–62.

89 *War* 1. 270; *Ant.* 14. 365–6.

90 *War* 1. 273.

91 *War* 1. 282–5; *Ant.* 14. 381–93.

92 *War* 1. 290–302; *Ant.* 14. 14. 394–41.

93 *War* 1. 328–44; *Ant.* 14. 41–64.

94 *Ant.* 14. 481.

95 *War* 1.354–7; *Ant.* 14. 387–91; 15. 9.

96 Matth 2:1; Luke 1:5.

97 Matth 2:5–6.

98 Luke 2:1–7.

99 See the fuller discussion in Part Three.

100 See Schürer-Vermes-Millar, *History* I (1973) pp. 413–16.

101 See Schürer-Vermes-Millar, *History* I (1973) pp. 399–427.

102 See Schürer-Vermes-Millar, *History* II (1979) pp. 598–606. The name 'Sicarii' or dagger men derives from the Latin *sica*, dagger, a weapon they always carried hidden under their cloaks.

103 See note 173.

104 See Schürer-Vermes-Millar, *History* I (1973) pp. 287–329, Peter Richardson, *Herod. King of the Jews and Friend of the Romans* (1999).

105 *Anchor Dictionary of the Bible* III (ed. D. Freedman, Yale University Press, New Haven, 2007, p. 989).

106 See mShabbat 24:3; mHullin 12:1. See E. D. Oren, 'Herodian Doves in the light of recent Archaeological Discoveries' (*Palestine Exploration Quarterly* 100, 1968) pp. 56–61.

107 On Josephus, see Tessa Rajak, *Josephus: The Historian and his Society* (Duckworth, London, 2nd ed., 2002).

108 Codex 50, folio 2r from the Burgerbibliothek of Berne in Switzerland.

109 See Schürer-Vermes-Millar, *History* I (1973) pp. 28–32.

110 Josephus, *Life* 1–6.

111 *Ant.* 16. 184–7.

112 *Ant.* 15. 174.

113 *Ant.* 15. 425; bTaanit 23a.

114 *Ant.* 18. 130, 133, 136.

115 Herod Antipas: Mt 14:1, 3, 6; Mk 6:14, 16–18, 20–22; 8:15; Lk 3:1, 19; 8:3; 9:7, 9; 13:21; 23:7–8, 11–12, 15; Acts 4:27; 13:1. Herod Agrippa I: Acts 12:1, 6, 11, 19, 21.

116 *Ant.* 20. 104.

117 E. Baltrusch, *Herodes* (Beck, Munich, 2011) p. 327.

118 *War* 1. 181.

119 *Ant.* 17. 191.

120 *Ant.* 13. 257.

121 *Ant.* 14. 403.

122 *Ant.* 14. 9.

123 See section on Herod, the builder, in Chapter 6.

124 *Saturae* 5. 180. See M. Stern, *Greek and Latin Authors on Jews and Judaism* (Israel Academy of Sciences and Humanities, Jerusalem, vol. I, no. 190) pp. 435–7.

125 See W. Dittenberger, OGIS (*Orientis Graeci Inscriptiones Selectae*) I, 415 (Leipzig, 1903).

126 *Ant.* 14. 8–269.

127 *War* 1. 193, 197.

128 *Ant.* 14. 137.

129 *War* 1. 194; *Ant.* 14. 137.

130 *War* 1. 218–22; *Ant.* 14. 271–6.

131 *War* 1. 226–35; *Ant.* 14. 281–92.

132 Nicolas of Damascus, *Autobiography*, Fragment 135, ed. Edith Parmentier et al., *Nicolas de Damas* (Les Belles Lettres, Paris, 2011, p. 304). See M. Stern, *Greek and Latin Authors on Jews and Judaism*, I (Israel Academy of Sciences and Humanities, Jerusalem, 1974) pp. 248–9.

133 *War* 1. 199–203.

134 *War* 1. 208–15; *Ant.* 14. 163–84.

135 *Ant.* 14. 172–6.

136 *Ant.* 15. 370.

137 *Ant.* 15. 373–9. The hypothesis that the 'Herodians' of the New Testament (Mark 3:6; 12:13) were Essenes has recently been revived by Joan Taylor in *The Essenes, the Scrolls and the Dead Sea* (Oxford University Press, Oxford, 2012) pp. 116–21.

138 *Ant.* 14. 127.

139 *War* 1. 225; *Ant.* 14. 280.

140 *War* 1. 243–4; *Ant.* 14. 324–6.

141 *War* 1. 248–52; *Ant.* 14. 330–36.

142 See above, pp. 54–55.

143 *War* 1. 270; *Ant.* 14. 366.

144 *Ant.* 14. 370.

145 *War* 1. 282–5; *Ant.* 14. 381–93.

146 *War* 1. 345–6.

147 *War* 1.354–7; *Ant.* 14. 14. 487–91. See Chapter 4.

148 *Ant.* 15. 3.

149 Schürer-Vermes-Millar, *History* I (1973) pp. 298–300, n. 36.

150 *Ant.* 15. 97.

151 *Ant.* 15. 100–03.

152 *Ant.* 15. 22, 40. In addition to Ananel, Herod created five further High Priests: Simon, son of Boethus, whose daughter Mariamme II became Herod's fourth wife after Doris, Mariamme I and Malthace (*Ant.* 15. 320–22); Jesus, son of Phiabi (*Ant.* 15. 322); Matthias, son of Theophilus (*Ant.* 17. 164–66); Joseph, son of Ellem (*Ant.* 17. 166) and Joazar, son of Boethus, Herod's brother-in-law, Mariamme's brother (*Ant.* 17. 164).

153 *Ant.* 15. 23–27.

154 *Ant.* 15. 56.

155 *Ant.* 15. 62–7.

156 *Ant.* 15. 85.

157 *Ant.* 15. 81.

158 *Ant.* 15. 227–9.

159 *Ant.* 15. 232–6.

160 *Ant.* 15. 236–9.

161 *Ant.* 15. 241–6.

162 *Ant.* 15. 247–52.

163 *Carmina*, 1. 37, 21.

164 *Ant.* 15. 193; *War* 1. 390.

165 *War* 1. 391.

166 *Ant.* 15. 331.

167 *Ant.* 15. 335–55.

168 *Ant.* 15. 342.

169 *Ant.* 19. 329.

170 *Ant.* 15. 292, 296–7.

171 *War* 1. 266–7; *Ant.* 14. 352–3.

172 See Avner Ecker, 'Dining with Herod', in *Herod the Great* ed. by Silvia Rozenberg & David Mevorah (The Israel Museum, Jerusalem, 2013) pp. 66–79.

173 During the rebellion between 66 and 70 CE, the revolutionary Sicarii-Zealots occupied Masada and continued to fight even after the fall of Jerusalem in 70 CE. Masada was excavated between 1965 and 1967 by an Israeli team of archaeologists under the direction of Yigael Yadin. Close to 1000 written documents and potsherds inscribed in Hebrew, Aramaic, Greek and Latin were discovered in the ruins. They comprise biblical extracts, a fragmentary scroll of the Wisdom of Ben Sira, the Song of the Holocaust of the Sabbath found also among the Dead Sea Scrolls, and as a real oddity, a small papyrus fragment of what is probably the oldest evidence of the Aeneid of the Latin poet, Virgil, and more than 4000 coins. See Yigael Yadin, *Masada* (Weidenfeld & Nicolson, London, 1966). *Masada I: The Aramaic and Hebrew Ostraca and Jar Inscriptions* ed. by Y, Yadin and J. Naveh; *The Coins of Masada* ed. by Y. Meshorer (Israel Exploration Society, Jerusalem, 1989). *Masada II: The Latin and Greek Documents* ed. by H.M. Cotton and J. Geiger (Israel Exploration Society, Jerusalem, 1989). *Masada V: Art and Architecture* ed. by G. Foerster (Israel Exploration Society, Jerusalem, 1996).

174 J. Magness, *The Archaeology of the Holy Land* (CUP, New York, 2012) p. 210.

175 *Ant.* 17. 162.

176 H.M. Cotton et al., *Corpus Inscriptionum Iudaeae/Palestinae*, vol. I, no. 54 (De Gruyter, Berlin, 2010) pp. 97–8. It is interesting to note that the ossuary contained in addition to Simon's remains those of a woman, no doubt his wife, and, unusually, the bones of their dog, indicating that there existed animal lovers among ancient Jews.

177 Hannah M. Cotton et al. (eds), *Corpus Inscriptionum Iudaeae/Palaestinae Volume I: Jerusalem. Part 1* (De Gruyter, Berlin/New York, 2010) pp. 42–5.

178 See *War* 5. 194.

179 *Ant.* 20. 219. For Agrippa II's role in finding jobs for 18,000 suddenly unemployed building workers, see Chapter 13.

180 *Ant.* 15. 268; 17. 255; *War* 2. 44.

181 For all the architectural details, see the posthumous essay of Ehud Netzer, 'Herod, Master Builder' in *Herod the Great* ed. by Silvia Rozenberg and David Mevorah (The Israel Museum, Jerusalem, 2013) pp. 80–117.

182 *Ant.* 15. 324.

183 Ehud Netzer, 'In Search of Herod's Tomb', *Biblical Archaeology Review* 37, January – February 2011, pp. 36–48; 'The Tomb Complex at Herodium' in *Herod the Great: The King's Final Journey* ed. by S. Rozenberg & D. Mevorah, pp. 240–65. 'The Sarcophagi from the Mausoleum unearthed at Herodium', ibid., pp. 266. See also the essay by E. Netzer et al. in *Herod the Great* ed. by Silvia Rozenberg and David Mevorah (The Israel Museum, Jerusalem, 2013) pp. 240–55.

184 *Ant.* 15. 331.

185 Jodi Magness, *The Archaeology of the Holy Land* (Cambridge University Press, New York, 2012) p. 172.

186 It may originally have commemorated the restoration of a lighthouse by Pontius Pilate, prefect of Judaea. See *Corpus Inscriptionum Iudaeae/Palaestinae*, vol. II, ed. by W. Ameling et al. (W. de Gruyter, Berlin, 2011, no. 1277) p. 278.

187 Acts 23:35.

188 Acts 25:13–26:32.

189 Cassius Dio, *History* 65.15. See Chapter 13.

190 *War* 1. 404; *Ant.* 15. 363. See J.F. Wilson, *Caesarea Philippi: Banias, the Lost City of Pan* (I.B. Tauris, London, 2004).

191 *War* 1. 426–7; *Ant.* 16. 149.

192 *War* 1. 477; *Ant.* 17. 14; mSanhedrin 2:4; CD 4:20–5:2; 11QTemple 57: 17–8. See G. Vermes, 'Sectarian Matrimonial Halakhah in the Damascus Rule', *JJS* 25 (1974) pp. 197–202.

193 See Chapter 8.

194 See Chapter 9.

195 See Figure 5.4.

196 *Ant.* 17. 58–9.

197 *Ant.* 16. 261–9.

198 *Ant.* 16. 513–32.

199 *Ant.* 16. 358–9.

200 *War* 1. 573; *Ant.* 17. 52–3.

201 *War* 1. 604–19; *Ant.*17. 79–92.

202 *War* 1. 661–5; *Ant.* 17. 182–91.

203 *Ant.* 17. 127–33.

204 *Ant.* 17. 151–63.

205 *Ant.* 17. 167. There was such an eclipse on 13 March 4 BCE.

206 *Ant.* 17. 168–69. Compare this with the picture of the demise of Agrippa I in Acts 12:23 and the death of Antiochus Epiphanes in 1 Mac 6:8–13.

Among modern medical diagnostic guesses figure cancer of the pancreas with thrombosis of the veins of the abdomen; cardiac failure and terminal uraemia with traumatic myiasis of the genitals. A clinic-pathological conference held at the University of Maryland in December 2012 came up with the suggestion that Herod's death was due to chronic kidney failure complicated by Fournier's gangrene of the testicles. Not a pleasant way to go.

207 *Ant.* 17. 171–2.

208 *War* 2. 10; *Ant.* 17. 213.

209 *War* 1. 660. It has been suggested that this story is fictional, simply illustrating the utter wickedness of a dying tyrant. But if the episode were pure invention of Josephus, the lesson would be much more striking if the account ended with the bloodbath of the imprisoned dignitaries.

210 *Ant.* 17.199.

211 *Ant.* 16. 248.

212 *Ant.* 17. 191.

213 See Schürer-Vermes-Millar, *History* I (1973) pp. 316–19.

214 *Melius est Herodis porcum esse quam filium.* Macrobius, *Saturnalia* 2. 4. 11 in M. Stern, *Greek and Latin Authors on Jews and Judaism*, vol. II, no. 543, pp. 665–6. The original of the saying was probably in Greek with the punning use of *hus* (pig) and *huios* (son).

215 *Ant.* 16. 150–1.

216 *Ant.* 16. 153.

217 *Ant.* 17. 191–2.

218 *Ant.* 15. 330.

219 *Ant.* 15. 309–10.

220 *Ant.* 17. 190.

221 *Ant.* 16.154–155.

222 *War* 1. 61; *Ant.* 7. 393; 13. 249.

223 *Ant.* 16. 179–88.

224 *Ant.* 16. 156–8.

225 *Ant.* 15. 379. Herod's liking for the Essenes was motivated by the prediction attributed to their prophet, Menahem, who after meeting the young Herod, assured the young man that one day he would be the king of the Jews (*Ant.* 15. 374).

      Herod's importance in the history of the Essenes is strongly emphasized by Joan Taylor. She believes that members of the community first came to Qumran during the early years of Herod's reign and suggests, on the basis of a loose interpretation of Philo's words, 'Great kings look upon them with admiration and amazement, and the approbation and honours which they give add further veneration to their venerable name' (Hypothetica 11. 18), that the land on which the Qumran buildings were erected was a gift by Herod to the Essenes. See *The Essenes, the Scrolls and the Dead Sea* (Oxford University Press, Oxford, 2012) pp. 45–6, 109–30, 247–8. Against this interesting surmise one should set the complete absence of allusions to Herod in the Dead Sea Scrolls themselves.

226 bSukkah 51b; bBaba Batra 4a.

227 S. Mason, *Josephus and the New Testament* (Hendrickson, Peabody, MA, 2nd ed., 2003) p. 152.

228 It seems that recently even Steve Mason has come to a more balanced and mature assessment of Herod's achievements. See his contribution 'Herod's Final Curtain: What to do for an Encore?' in *Herod the Great* ed. by S. Rozenberg & D. Mevorah, pp. 45–54.

229 *The Herods of Judaea* (Clarendon Press, Oxford, 1938) pp. 153–4.

230 A. Schalit, *König Herodes: Der Mann, und sein Werk* (W. de Gruyter, Berlin, 1969) pp. 664–75.

231 E. Baltrusch, in *Herodes* (Beck, Munich, 2011).

232 Schalit also uses the phrases 'tragic error' and 'tragic destiny' in connection with Herod in *König Herodes* (W. de Gruyter, Berlin, 1969) pp. 671 and 674, and Baltrusch thinks along the same lines, too in *Herodes* (Beck, Munich, 2011) p. 333.

233 Matth 2:8.

234 Naseeb Shaheen, *Biblical Reference in Shakespeare's Plays* (University of Delaware Press, Newark, 1999) p. 193.

235 *Ant.* 15. 97.

236 *Ant.* 15. 97–103. Cleopatra was thinking of seducing Herod and thereby infuriating Antony who would take bloody revenge on the Jewish king. Herod in turn was not unwilling to get rid of Cleopatra, but his friends dissuaded him from doing so.

237 Matth 2:13–18. See G. Vermes, *The Nativity: History and Legend* (Penguin, London, 2006, pp. 116–28).

238 Ps.-Philo, *Book of Biblical Antiquities* 9. 10.

239 Exodus Rabbah 1:22; bSotah 13a; bMegillah 14a.

240 *Ant.* 2. 205.

241 2 Timothy 3:8.

242 CD 5:18.

243 Targum Pseudo-Jonathan on Exodus 1:15.

244 *War* 2. 1–98; 111–17. *Ant.* 17. 317–21; 342–4. See Schürer-Vermes-Millar, *History* I (1973) pp. 353–57.

245 Luke 1:26; 2:39.

246 See Schürer-Vermes-Millar, *History* I (1973) pp. 330–35.

247 See Introduction to Part Two.

248 *War* 2. 2; *Ant.* 18. 2. On the Roman governors (*praefecti*) and their powers, see Schürer-Vermes-Millar, *History* I (1973) pp. 357–99.

249 Schürer-Vermes-Millar, *History* I (1973) pp. 484–613.

250 *War* 2. 167–8, 181–3; *Ant.* 18:27, 36–8, 101–29, 240–56. Mark 6:14–29; Matth 14:1–12; Luke 9:7–9; 23:6–12. See Schürer-Vermes-Millar, *History* I (1973) pp. 340–53.

251 Matth 14:1, 9.

252 See Schürer-Vermes-Millar, *History* I (1973) pp. 581–2.

253 Mark 6:17–29; Matth 14:3–12.

254 *Ant.* 18. 113–6.

255 *Ant.* 18:116–19.

256 *Ant.* 18. 116.

257 See Eric M. Meyers, Ehud Netzer, Carol L. Meyers: *Sepphoris* (Eisenbrauns, Winona Lake, 1992).

258 *Ant.* 18. 27.

259 John 6:23.

260 John 6:1; 21:1.

261 Luke 23:7.

262 Luke 9:7.

263 Luke 9:9; 13:31–2.

264 Luke 23:6–11.

265 *War* 2. 183; *Ant.* 18. 252.

266 Luke 3:1.

267 See R. Arav & R.A. Freund, *Bethsaida: A City by the North Shore of the Sea of Galilee* (Truman State University Press, Kirksville, MO, 1995–2004).

268 *Ant.* 18. 108.

269 Matth 16:13; Mark 8:27.

270 *Ant.* 18. 106–7.

271 *War* 2. 178–82; 206–22; *Ant.* 18. 143–239; 19. 274–359; Acts 12: 1–23. See Schürer-Vermes-Millar, *History* I (1973) pp. 442–54.

272 *Ant.* 19. 338–42.

273 mSotah 7:8.

274 *Ant.* 20. 104.

275 Acts 12:1–23.

276 *Ant.* 19. 343–52.

277 *War* 2. 221–2; *Ant.* 20. 103–4.

278 *Ant.* 18–20; Acts 25–26. Schürer-Vermes-Millar, *History* I (1973) pp. 471–83.

279 *Life* 365.

280 *Against Apion* 1. 51.

281 *Ant.* 20. 104.

282 *Ant.* 20. 145.

283 'Finally a diamond of great renown, made precious by the finger of Bernice. It was given as a present long ago by the barbarian Agrippa to his incestuous sister, in that country where kings celebrate festal Sabbaths with bare feet, and where a long established clemency suffers pigs to attain old age.' Juvenal, *Saturae* 6. 156–60. Translation by G.G. Ramsay in the Loeb Classical Library.

284 Tacitus, *Hist.* 2, 2, 1.

285 'On account of his notorious passion for Queen Berenice, to whom, it was said, he even proposed marriage' (Suetonius, *Divus Titus* 7. 1–2).

286 Jean Racine, Bérénice (1670); Pierre Corneille, *Tite et Bérénice* (1670). The English poet laureate John Masefield also wrote in 1922 a play entitled *Berenice*.

287 Antonio Cesti & Nicola Beregani, *Il Tito* (1660); Antonio Caldara & Carlo Sigismondo Capace, *Tito e Berenice* (1714); Giuseppe Maria Orlandini & Benedetto Pasqualigo, *Berenice* (1725), and so on.

288 Act 26: 24–32. Credulous Christian interpreters of the Acts take these words in the literal sense and imagine that Agrippa was on the point of becoming a Christian convert.

289 *Assumption or Testament of Moses* 6:2 (*rex petulans*). See J. Priest in J.H. Charlesworth, *The Old Testament Pseudepigrapha* I (Darton, Longman & Todd, London, 1983) p. 930.

290 bBaba Batra 3ab.

291 Matth 2; Luke 2. See G. Vermes, *The Nativity* (Penguin, London, 2006); *Jesus: Nativity – Passion – Resurrection* (Penguin, London, 2010).

Bibliography

Greek critical edition of Josephus

Flavii Josephi opera I–VII, ed. by Benedict Niese (Weidmann, Berlin, 1885–1895)

Greek-English text of Josephus

Josephus, *The Life. Against Apion*, translated by H. St. J. Thackeray (William Heinemann, London/ Harvard University Press, Cambridge, MA, 1926)
—— *The Jewish War, Books I–III*, translated by H. St. J. Thackeray (William Heinemann, London/ Harvard University Press, Cambridge, MA, 1956)
—— *Judean War 2. Translation and Commentary* by Steve Mason (Brill, Leiden, 2008)
—— *Jewish Antiquities, Books XII–XIV, XV–XVII*, translated by Ralph Marcus (William Heinemann, London/Harvard University Press, Cambridge, MA, 1957, 1963)

English Translations

The Works of Flavius Josephus, translated by William Whiston (William P. Nimmo, Edinburgh, 1865)
—— *The Life of Herod from the* Jewish Antiquities *of Josephus*, translated by John Gregory. Introduced by Martin Goodman (Everyman, J.M. Dent, London, 1998)
—— *Life of Herod*, translated from the Greek by John Gregory. Introduced by Martin Goodman (The Folio Society, London, 2007)

Greek-French text of Nicholas of Damascus

Nicolas de Damas, *Histoires – Receuil de coutumes – Vie d'Auguste – Autobiographie*. Textes traduits et commentés par Edith Parmentier et Francesca Prometea Barone (Les Belles Lettres, Paris, 2011)

Classical sources in English

Suetonius, *The Twelve Caesars*, translated by Robert Graves (Penguin Classics, London, 2007)
Tacitus, *Annals*, translated by Michael Grant (Penguin Classics, London, 2003)
—— *The Histories*, translated by W. H. Fyfe (Penguin Classics, London, 2009)

Studies

Arav, R. & Freund, R.A., *Bethsaida: A City by the North Shore of the Sea of Galilee* (Truman State University Press, Kirksville, MO, 1995–2004)
Ariel, D.T. & Fontanille, J.P., *The Coins of Herod* (Brill, Leiden, 2012)
Avi-Yonah, M. & Baras, Z., 'The Herodian Period' in *World History of the Jewish People*, vol. I, vii (Rutgers University Press, New Brunswick, 1975)
Baltrusch, Ernst, *Herodes: König im Heiligen Land. Eine Biographie* (C.H. Beck, Munich, 2012)
Barnes, T.D., 'The Date of Herod's Death' (*Journal of Theological Studies* 19, 1968) pp. 204–9
Bickerman, Elias, 'The Warning Inscription of Herod's Temple', in *Studies in Jewish and Christian History, Part Two* (Brill, Leiden, 1980) pp. 210–24
Bowersock, G., *Roman Arabia* (Harvard University Press, Cambridge, MA, 1983)
Braund, David, 'Greek and Roman Authors on the Herods', in *The World of the Herods* by N. Kokkinos (Franz Steiner, Stuttgart, 2007) pp. 35–44
Fuks, Gideon, 'Josephus on Herod's Attitude to the Jewish Religion: the Darker Side' (*JJS* 53, 2002) pp. 238–45
Goodman, Martin, *The Roman World 44 BC – AD 180* (Routledge, London, 1997)
Grant, Michael, *Herod the Great* (Weidenfeld & Nicolson, London, 1971)
Hoehner, H., *Herod Antipas, a Contemporary of Jesus Christ* (Cambridge University Press, Cambridge, 1972)
Jacobson, David M. & Kokkinos, Nikos (eds), *Herod and Augustus. Papers Presented at the Institute of Jewish Studies Conference, 21st – 23rd June 2005* (Brill, Leiden, 2009)
Jones, A.H.M., *The Herods of Judaea* (Clarendon Press, Oxford, 1938, reprinted 1967)

Kasher, A. & Witzum, E., *King Herod: A Persecuted Persecutor: A Case Study in Psychohistory and Psychobiography* (De Gruyter, Berlin, 2007)

Kokkinos, Nikos, *The Herodian Dynasty: Origins, Role in Society and Eclipse* (Sheffield Academic Press, Sheffield, 1998)

—— 'Herod's Horrid Death' (*BAR* 28/2, 2002) pp. 28–35, 62

—— 'The Prefects of Judaea 6–48 CE and the Coins from the Misty Period' in *Judaea and Rome in Coins 65 BCE–135 CE*, ed. by D.M. Jacobson & N. Kokkinos (Spink, London, 2012) pp. 85–111

Kokkinos, Nikos (ed.), *The World of the Herods and the Nabataeans* (Franz Steiner, Stuttgart, 2007)

Mahieu, B., *Between Rome and Jerusalem: Herod the Great and his Sons in their Struggle for Recognition. A Chronological Investigation of the Period 40 BC–39 AD, with a Time Setting of New Testament Events* (Peeters, Leuven, 2012)

Mason, Steve, *Josephus and the New Testament* (Hendrickson, Peabody, MA, 2nd ed., 2003)

Meshorer, Ya'akov, *Jewish Coins from the Second Temple Period* (Am Hassefer & Massada, Tel-Aviv, 1967)

—— *A Treasury of Jewish Coins. From the Persian Period to Bar Kokhba* (Amphora Books, Amsterdam, 2001)

Meyers, Eric M., Netzer, Ehud, Meyers Carol L., *Sepphoris* (Eisenbrauns, Winona Lake, 1992)

Millar, Fergus, *The Roman Near East 31 BC – AD 337* (Harvard University Press, Cambridge, MA, 1993)

Netzer, Ehud, *The Palaces of the Hasmoneans and Herod the Great* (Yad Izhak Ben-Zvi Publications, Jerusalem, 2001)

Netzer, E. & Laureys-Chachy, R., *The Architecture of Herod, the Great Builder* (Mohr Siebeck, Tübingen, 2006)

Otto, W., *Herodes: Beiträge zur Geschichte der letzten jüdischen Königshauses* (Stuttgart, 1913)

Pucci Ben Zeev, M., *Jewish Rights in the Roman World: The Greek and Roman Documents quoted by Josephus Flavius* (Mohr Siebeck, Tübingen, 1998)

Rajak, Tessa, *Josephus: The Historian and his Society* (Duckworth, London, 2nd ed., 2002)

—— 'Josephus as Historian of the Herods', in *The World of the Herods* by N. Kokkinos (Franz Steiner, Stuttgart 2007) pp. 23–34

Richardson, Peter, *Herod, King of the Jews and Friend of the Romans* (Fortress Press, Minneapolis, 1999)

Rocca, S., *Herod's Judaea: A Mediterranean State in the Classical World* (Mohr Siebeck, Tübingen, 2008)

Rozenberg, S. & Mevorah, D., *Herod the Great: The King's Final Journey* (The Israel Museum, Jerusalem, 2013)

Sandmel, Samuel, *Herod: Profile of a Tyrant* (Lipincott, Philadelphia, 1967)

Schalit, Abraham, *König Herodes: Der Mann und sein Werk* [King Herod: the Man and his Work] (Walter de Gruyter, Berlin, 1969)

Schürer, Emil, Vermes, Geza & Millar, Fergus, *The History of the Jewish People in the Age of Jesus Christ*, vol. I (T. & T. Clark, Edinburgh, 1973) pp. 287–329; 336–483

Schwartz, D.R., *Agrippa I. The Last King of Judaea* (Mohr Siebeck, Tübingen, 1990)
—— 'Herod in Ancient Jewish Literature' in *The World of the Herods* by N. Kokkinos (Franz Steiner, Stuttgart, 2007) pp. 45–53
Sievers, J., *Synopsis of the Greek Sources for the Hasmonaean Period: 1–2 Maccabees and Josephus, War 1 and Antiquities 12–14* (Ponificio Istituto Biblico, Rome, 2001)
Smallwood, E.M., *The Jews under Roman Rule* (Brill, Leiden, 1976).
Stern, Menahem, 'A. Schalit's Herod' (*JJS* 11, 1960) pp. 49–58
—— 'The Reign of Herod and the Herodian Dynasty', in *The Jewish People in the First Century I*, ed. by S. Safrai & M. Stern (an Gorcum, Assen, 1974) pp. 216–307
—— *Greek and Latin Authors on Jews and Judaism*, Vol. I–III (Israel Academy of Sciences and Humanities, Jerusalem, 1980–84)
Syme, Ronald, *The Roman Revolution* (Oxford University Press, Oxford, 1939)
Taylor, Joan E., *The Essenes, the Scrolls and the Dead Sea* (Oxford University Press, Oxford, 2012)
Vermes, Geza, *Who's Who in the Age of Jesus* (Penguin, London, 2005)
—— *The Nativity: History and Legend* (Penguin, London, 2006. ix, 177 pp.)
—— *Jesus: Nativity – Passion – Resurrection* (Penguin, London, 2010, x, 482 pp.)
—— 'Herod the Terrible or Herod the Great?' (*Standpoint*, January–February 2011) pp. 86–93
—— *The Complete Dead Sea Scrolls in English* (Penguin, London, 2011, xxii, 698 pp., 50th anniversary edition)
Vörös, Győző, 'Machaerus where Salome Danced and John the Baptist was Beheaded' (*BAR* 38/5, 2012) pp. 30–41, 68
Wilson, John F., *Caesarea Philippi: Banias, the Lost City of Pan* (I.B. Tauris, London, 2004)
Yadin, Yigael, *Masada, Herod's Fortress and the Zealots' Last Stand* (Weidenfeld & Nicolson, London, 1966)

Image credits and copyrights

4.8   Image courtesy of vcoins.

5.1   Image courtesy of Numismatica Ars Classica.

5.2   Bloomsbury Academic.

5.3   Robert Harding Picture Library/SuperStock.

5.4   Bloomsbury Academic.

5.5   William Storage, !STORAX.

6.1   Public domain.

6.2   British Museum.

6.3   Bloomsbury Academic.

6.4   Amit Erez, Jerusalem at night, amite.photoshelter.com

6.5   Deror avi, via Wikimedia Commons.

6.6   Hanan Isachar, *isachar-photography.photoshelter.com/*

6.7   Godot13, via Wikimedia Commons.

6.8   Hanan Isachar, *isachar-photography.photoshelter.com/*

6.9   Todd Bolen/BiblePlaces.com

6.10 Getty images, Romulo Rejon.

6.11 Zev Radovan, www.biblelandpictures.com/

6.12 Ariely, via Wikimedia Commons.

6.13 Bloomsbury Academic.

6.14 Holy Land Photos.

6.15 Bloomsbury Academic.

6.16 Todd Bolen/BiblePlaces.com

6.17 Todd Bolen/BiblePlaces.com

6.18 Hanan Isachar, *isachar-photography.photoshelter.com/*

6.19 Todd Bolen/BiblePlaces.com

6.20 Bloomsbury Academic.

6.21 Istock/Kavram.

6.22 Zeev Weiss.

6.23 The Israel Museum, Jerusalem.

6.24 www.biblewalks.com

6.25 Todd Bolen/BiblePlaces.com

7.1   David Bivin/www.LifeintheHolyLand.com

7.2   The Israel Museum, Jerusalem.

7.3   The Israel Museum, Jerusalem.

I.1   Superstock.

I.2   The Bridgeman Art Library.

I.3   Zev Radovan, www.biblelandpictures.com/

I.4   Superstock.

8.1   Image courtesy of vcoins.

9.1   Public domain.

9.2   Image courtesy of CNG Coins, www.cngcoins.com

9.3   Superstock.

9.4   Album/Joseph Martin, Superstock.

9.5   Todd Bolen/BiblePlaces.com

9.6   Courtesy of the Israel Antiquities Authority/Zeev Weiss.

9.7   PierreSelim, via Wikimedia Commons.

10.1 Todd Bolen/BiblePlaces.com

10.2 Image courtesy of CNG Coins, www.cngcoins.com

11.1 British Museum.

11.2 Image courtesy of CNG Coins, www.cngcoins.com

12.1 Image courtesy of CNG Coins, www.cngcoins.com

13.1 Image courtesy of CNG Coins, www.cngcoins.com

13.2 DeAgostini/Superstock.

13.3 Iberfoto/Superstock.

13.4 Album/Prisma/Superstock.

Index

Page numbers in *italics* refer to illustrations. All references to 'Herod' refer to the main subject of the book; other characters with the name 'Herod' are distinguished with additional information.